GHOSTS AND LEGENDS OF GENESEE & LAPEER COUNTIES

ROXANNE RHOADS AND JOE SCHIPANI

Haunted America

Published by Haunted America,
A Division of The History Press
Charleston, SC
www.historypress.com

First published 2022

Manufactured in the United States

ISBN 9781467149945

Library of Congress Control Number: 2022937894

In Loving Memory of
ClaraBelle Rebecca (Harwood) Casey
October 30, 1937–February 25, 2021

CONTENTS

PREFACE

Ghosts bridge the past to the present; they speak across the seemingly insurmountable barriers of death and time, connecting us to what we thought was lost. They give us hope for a life beyond death and because of this help us to cope with loss and grief. Their presence is the promise that we don't have to say goodbye to our loved ones right away.

—*Colin Dickey,* Ghostland: An American History in Haunted Places

I dedicated this book to my mother, who passed away unexpectedly while we were working on it. She's the reason I have always been interested in ghosts and the paranormal. She taught me there is more to this world than what we can see and that our spirits live on after the physical body dies. She always spoke of spirits with a no-nonsense manner, just like she would speak of someone corporeal standing next to us.

I am pretty sure she was a medium or at the least clairsentient. She would ask for help, and they would guide her way. After someone passed, she always expected to receive a sign that they were OK on the other side. She always received a sign.

When she passed away suddenly in February 2021, I was shocked and utterly wrecked by grief. After her death, I kept expecting her to send me a sign that everything was OK. But she didn't.

At least, I didn't think she did.

I was expecting something flashy like seeing her translucent figure on her porch waving to me as I looked out the window and across the yard that separated our homes.

But that's not how it works. As the weeks wore on, I realized she had been sending signs and communicating with us the entire time. She sent my daughter directly to a drawer that contained all of her "in case of emergency" information, including her will and life insurance paperwork. She also sent my daughter into the basement to grab a box I was desperate to find—it contained love letters my grandparents had written to each other. My daughter said she had no idea how she knew where the box was, it was like her grandma had guided her directly to it.

I finally realized she was sending messages to me when I was going through a pile of papers and found a tiny folded slip of paper from a notepad, probably only about three by four inches. It was mixed into a pile of other papers, and I almost threw it in the trash. On the paper were random notes, names and phone numbers. At first, it didn't look like anything important.

But on the bottom she had written:

> *Francis Plourde—shot and put in freezer in his store on Pierson Rd in the 1970s.*

This was the clue I needed for my research. I had been looking for these details forever. That name was what I needed to point me in the right direction. I sent it to Joe, and he was able to pull up the old newspaper clippings. I couldn't believe it. That note had nothing to do with anything else on that little piece of paper. She sent me that clue. Even after death she helped me.

As I continued to sort through her things, I found a *Flint Journal* clipping from the Plourde murder in an envelope. I almost tossed it in the trash with the piles of junk mail, but something told me to look inside. It contained a newspaper article that had more details than the online snippets from other newspapers. Once again, she helped me.

Even after death, she was there, answering my questions and sending me clues.

—Roxanne

ACKNOWLEDGMENTS

Thanks to COVID, Joe and I hit many roadblocks while working on this book. All the historical societies were closed, and the Flint Public Library was closed for renovations; access was limited at its temporary location. We had to make do with the historical archives we could use online and what information we could coax from the locations and the people willing to talk to us. If you were one of those people, thank you, we appreciate you so much.

A huge thank-you goes out to Justin Arnold, who provided invaluable information about his hometown of Lapeer. He helped immensely not only in pointing out locations to research but also offered details about his own otherworldly experiences.

Thank you to my Obsidian sisters Samantha Groom and Laura Bickle for listening to my drama and offering support. A big thanks to Sam for sharing historical details about Crossroads Village and for being my personal tour guide during our visits there.

Thank you to my bestie, Ilona Curry, who always had my back during this book's creation, even helping with everyday aspects of life like picking up The Kid from school so I had more time and energy to devote to the book.

Thank you to my kids Ari and Robby for always being excited to visit haunted locations with me, and thank you to my husband, Robert, for visiting spooky places with me when the kids weren't available. I love you guys.

Thank you to my son Tim and his significant other, Bre, for all their love and support.

And last but not least, thank you to Dr. Thomas Aaberg for preserving my sight so I could complete this book.

—Roxanne

To my partner, Phillip, thank you for always supporting my crazy endeavors over the last fifteen years and motivating me to live my best life.

I would like to thank Kay, Michael and Wanda from the Flint Public Library for allowing me access to the microfilm during your remodel and everything else that was going on. I would also like to thank my children and grandchildren for making my life better.

—Joe

Introduction

*Hauntings keep alive neglected spaces and make them relevant
to their communities once again.*

—*Colin Dickey*, Ghostland: An American History in Haunted Places

Spooky stories and terrifying tales lurk in dark rural corners and on historic main streets throughout Genesee and Lapeer Counties. Hospitals, cemeteries and historic homes have numerous ghosts attached to them.

The secrets of the dead can be buried in history, but we like to dig into the archives and coax the stories back to life, if only for a fleeting moment, with words on the page.

Several chapters in this book feature locations where history, true crime and the paranormal intersect. These sinister tales of murder have led to locations full of paranormal activity. A Clio man's spirit is thought to still reside in the junkyard office where he was murdered. The incident was billed as the internet's first murder case and made nationwide headlines as the Instant Message Murder.

For almost two centuries, the Flushing area has been fascinated by tales of the wealthy Brent family whose land is connected to numerous tales of murder, mystery and ghosts. The land may also have ties to the brutal 1928 murder of five-year-old Dorothy Schneider.

The Lapeer State Home has ties to unethical medical practices, eugenics and murder. The land and remaining buildings that once belonged to the home are considered to be extremely haunted.

We dive into the history and uncover the dark truths that have led to such haunting tales. We hope you enjoy this tour of Genesee and Lapeer Counties' most haunted locations.

1
GHOSTS OF VEHICLE CITY (FLINT)

We are all haunted
The past is always with us
Ghosts are everywhere

—haiku by Roxanne Rhoads

Flint is the birthplace of General Motors. It became known as the Vehicle City, first because of the multiple carriage companies located in Flint, then later when Flint became a city world renowned for automotive innovation.

It all started in 1855 when the small but prosperous village of Flint officially became a city with around two hundred residents. By the end of the nineteenth century, Flint had become the center of Michigan's lumber industry. The city reached its peak as a lumbering town in 1870. As the lumber industry boomed, the next industry, transportation, emerged. Carts, wagons and carriages were needed for transporting lumber along with lumber workers and their families. In 1869, the first major carriage factory opened. Incorporated in 1896, the W.A. Paterson Company grew into a three-building complex spanning across Saginaw and Harrison Streets.

In the early 1880s, Flint Wagon Works was founded. James H. Whiting, manager of the Begole Fox lumber business, suggested the company make wagons. He partnered with Josiah W. Begole, David S. Fox, George L. Walker and Allen Beach Sr. to set up shop on Flint's West Kearsley Street in a vacant Begole Fox lumberyard.

The Flint Cotton & Woolen Mills Company built a new cotton mill on Water Street in 1880. In 1886, Josiah Dallas Dort and Billy Durant bought the Coldwater Cart Company and moved it to Flint, leasing the cotton mill building that had closed earlier that year. They renamed the business the Flint Road Cart Company, and by the end of their first year in business, Dort and Durant had produced four thousand vehicles. In 1896, they renamed the company, incorporated as the Durant-Dort Carriage Company and built headquarters across the street from their factory in what is now known as the Carriage Town area of Flint. By 1900, Durant-Dort Carriage Company had become the number-one producer of horse-drawn carriages in the country. The "Blue Ribbon" carriages made Durant and Dort millionaires.

Flint Wagon Works, the W.A. Paterson Company and the Durant-Dort Carriage Company were the original Big Three.

In the early twentieth century, Flint was a successful automobile manufacturing city. Business was booming, and men from all over the United States came to Flint for manufacturing jobs. In 1900, Flint was producing over 100,000 horse-drawn vehicles per year. Also in 1900, the horseless carriage was introduced to Flint when Judge Charles Wisner, a genius who patented five inventions and whose workshop still stands in the historical Crossroad's Village, drove Flint's first horseless carriage down Saginaw Street in the Labor Day Parade. The carriage moved like magic, wowing approximately 10,000 spectators before it eventually stuttered and stalled. But that ride lasted long enough to catch the eye of visionary Billy Durant. Durant did not buy Wisner's patent for the automobile, but the idea of a horseless carriage stuck in his head.

In late 1903, Flint Wagon Works, a rival of Durant and Dort, pushed the city into the automobile craze. President James H. Whiting decided to purchase David Buick's fledgling Buick Motor Company to build engines for farm equipment. David Dunbar Buick and his chief engineer, Walter Marr, stayed with the company and convinced Whiting to manufacture the first Buick motorcar. By 1904, Flint Wagon Works had begun producing automobiles, but the process was slow and costly. Whiting was frustrated. He dissolved the old Buick Motor Company and incorporated a completely new entity, The Buick Motor Company. Billy Durant then took over the management of Buick.

In June 1905, during Flint's fiftieth birthday golden jubilee celebration floats paraded down Saginaw Street depicting the evolution of the vehicle; buildings were dressed in red, white and blue buntings and flags; and two additional arches were added to downtown Flint. These new arches featured

Flint Arches postcard. *Author collection.*

the Vehicle City crown at their apex. The city of Flint officially became known as the Vehicle City.

Durant wished to lure Charles Stewart Mott to the Vehicle City. Mott was the president of the Weston-Mott Company in New York. Durant's charm worked, and in 1907, Mott moved his company to Flint and merged with The Buick Motor Company. During this time, the auto industry was booming, and everyone was coming to try their hand at a motorized fortune.

In 1908, Durant wanted to get a jump on all the competition. He founded General Motors in Flint so he would be able to consolidate all the companies under one umbrella. He then acquired Oldsmobile, Cadillac, Oakland (which became Pontiac) and various truck companies that were all merged into GMC. He also purchased A.C. Sparkplug and moved it from Boston to Flint. Also in 1908, Paterson joined the craze and began building the Paterson Automobile.

In 1910, Durant got into a financial bind and had to turn General Motors over to the banks because he was overextended. But that didn't stop him. He teamed up with race car driver Louis Chevrolet to form the Chevrolet Motor Company in 1911. That year, the Dalton Automobile Company was started by Huber Dalton.

Ever the entrepreneur, Billy Durant added more companies to his résumé in 1914 when he formed the Monroe Motor Company with R.F. Monroe from Pontiac. Both Monroe and Chevrolet vehicles were manufactured in the Chevrolet Factory. Vehicle City was now cranking out Buick, Chevrolet, Paterson, Dalton, Wey, Whiting and Monroe automobiles in addition to trucks and carriages.

Thanks to Chevrolet's popularity, Durant was able to take back control of GM in 1916. In 1919, Durant hired Alfred P. Sloan and Charles F. Kettering to manage GM. Flint continued to see prosperity and growth, so much so that the famous arches were removed and traffic lights were installed. (In 2002, under the watchful eyes of the Genesee County Historical Society, new arches were erected along Saginaw Street to replicate the original look.)

But Durant's success was on a downward slope. In 1920, he lost GM for the final time. He founded Durant Motors in 1921 and built a huge factory on South Saginaw Street between Atherton and Hemphill. Durant Motors folded in 1931, and Durant went bankrupt in 1936. The factory sold to GM. This site became known as the Fisher Body Plant no. 1 and made bodies for Buick. When the Fisher Body plant closed in 1987, it was a major blow to Flint's economy and started a downward spiral Flint has never recovered from. Michael Moore made a documentary film about it titled *Roger & Me*.

Durant continued to invest in "the next big thing" throughout his life. He was a visionary and inventor, but not all ideas worked out financially. He died bankrupt in March 1947.

These men, who became known as automotive giants, left their mark on Flint. Now their names grace local buildings and street signs. The buildings where they lived and worked have historical markers in front of them. Bronze statues of the men themselves cast shadows across locations all over Flint. Several people have mentioned that they think the statues are haunted, that the eyes will follow you, especially the statues of Durant and Dort in Carriage Town. Local medium Davonna Wallace swears the statue of Otto Graff turned and smiled at her one morning on her way to work.

It's not a stretch to think that the spirits of these automotive giants still reside in Flint, the city they brought to life, the city where their businesses began. Their spirits linger, watching over the city they created, encouraging it to come back to life and once again become a place of innovation.

Phantoms of the auto industry continue to linger in Flint like a mist that never fully goes away. Some are simply shadowy remains of Flint's glory days, while others are solid reminders set in brick and stone-like Factory One and the Durant-Dort building.

During a haunted tour for the promotion of *Haunted Flint*, Roxanne and Joe visited the Durant-Dort Office Building in Carriage Town. The Durant-

Statues of Billy Durant and J. Dallas Dort. *Photo by Roxanne Rhoads.*

Dort Office Building is where automotive history was made. The location is heralded as the birthplace of General Motors—all the plans, plots and deals that Durant took part in happened in that building. Yet during the tour, it felt remarkably sterile. Anyone sensitive to such energies would think there

Left: Statue of Otto P. Graff. *Photo by Roxanne Rhoads.*

Below: Durant Dort Carriage Company, now home of the Genesee County Historical Society. *Photo by Roxanne Rhoads.*

would be huge amounts of energy and historical imprints in the place. But it felt like it had been scrubbed clean or possibly warded, as though, even long after death, the powerful men who worked in the building wanted their secrets to remain secret. Forever. Davonna Wallace, who was the medium on hand for the haunted tour, vocalized that idea; she felt that the building was remarkably empty. Such a historic location should be intricately laced with emotional history. The history should have been ingrained into the very foundation, especially considering the historical artifacts like original furniture, books and other items that remain in the building. We concluded that the men who made history with General Motors either knew enough about the arcane to scrub the building or to ward it so their secrets would remain safe throughout time.

The historical building has a few ghost stories attached to it.

A couple employees of the Durant-Dort have complained that lights are on when they know they turned them off or vice versa. Others who have worked in the building have heard ghostly footsteps and felt as though someone was behind them, but when they turned no one was there.

There is one story from someone who once worked in the building that is a little spookier:

> In the winter of 2006, an employee of the Flint Area Convention and Visitors Bureau arrived for work early one snowy morning. She was the first one there and went up to the second floor to get the coffee started. While making coffee, she heard the front door creak open downstairs and footsteps on the hard floor. She yelled "Good morning," but no one answered. When she looked down the staircase to see who had arrived, no one was there. She looked outside, and hers was still the only car in the lot and her footprints were the only ones in the snow.

Across from the Durant-Dort office building is Factory One, the first General Motors factory, which opened in 1886. It eventually was sold and housed many other businesses over the years. General Motors purchased the building in 2013 and began extensive renovations. In 2015, GM announced the building would feature an automotive archive and research center, along with a conference and event space that could accommodate groups of up to three hundred. Factory One held its grand opening in 2017.

Even after all the renovations, Factory One retains the ghosts of its past. Sometimes when the archive historian is alone, they hear footsteps pacing on the second floor. Back and forth, back and forth—this usually happens in

Above: Factory One. *Photo by Roxanne Rhoads.*

Opposite: Charles Nash House. *Photo by Roxanne Rhoads.*

the early morning hours or late in the evening. Sometimes current Factory One employees will smell industrial smoke and the odors of old machines. The factory parts are long gone, yet their spirit lives on in the first factory to build General Motors automobiles.

On Mason Street across from the Durant-Dort is a pretty Queen Anne–style house built around 1890. Locals refer to it as the pink house, the dollhouse or the Charles Nash house.

Charles W. Nash started working at the Flint Road Cart Company for one dollar a day in 1890 as a seat cushion stuffer. He advanced through the ranks quickly. Within six months, he became superintendent of the factory. Within ten years, Nash became vice president and general manager of the Durant-Dort Carriage Company. Nash was appointed vice president of Buick in 1910. In late 1912, Nash was elected as the fifth president of General Motors. Under his leadership, General Motors' profits skyrocketed. In 1916, Nash bought the Jeffery Motor Company of Kenosha, Wisconsin, best known for its Rambler brand. He renamed the

company Nash Motors in 1917. Nash passed away in 1948 at the age of eighty-four in Beverly Hills, California.

No one currently lives in the pretty Queen Anne. Over the years, it has gone through numerous owners who never seem to stay very long. Local Flint residents feel something is "off" about the house. They've seen odd shadows and movements in the empty house and feel a strong presence urging them to stay away.

2

A Spook in the Stacks

UM Flint's Thompson Library

The University of Michigan–Flint's Thompson Library opened in October 1994. It is odd for such a new building to be haunted, but consider the contents—thousands of old books that have been touched by many hands, artwork that spans the decades, and stacks of books and materials that thousands of students, professors and researchers have perused. Such a high-traffic area filled with strong emotion is bound to have at least a few residuals that can be seen by those who share the right energy frequency. Walking through isolated stacks in an empty library can always be a bit unnerving. You never know who or what could be lurking on the other side of that wall of books.

Librarians and other staff members at the Thompson Library claim there is at least one spook in the stacks at UM-Flint. Grant Burns, who was assistant director of the library until his death in 2006, loved to discuss the phantom page-turner with other staff members. He even wrote an article about "The Ghost in the Library" in the UM-Flint newspaper decades ago. Grant first encountered the spirit one Saturday while making his final rounds. Long after the last student had left the building, Grant suddenly heard pages frantically being turned. He thought perhaps some student was hiding in a quiet corner trying to complete research for an assignment, but after searching and searching, no one was found—yet the sound of turning pages was still heard.

Grant discussed the eerie encounter with other staff, who reported similar sounds. They have no idea who the ethereal scholar might be or where they

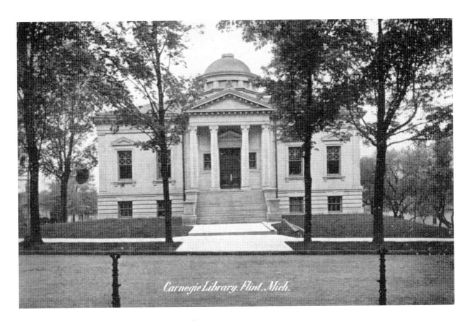

Carnegie Library postcard. *Author collection.*

came from. Grant even mused that their book-loving ghost may go back to the old Flint Public Library that stood right down the street from where the Thompson Library now stands. In the early 1900s, philanthropist Andrew Carnegie's grants led to over three thousand libraries being built throughout the world. In 1902, Flint was gifted a beautiful Carnegie library, which was located on the corner of East Kearsley and Clifford Streets (which no longer exists). The beautiful piece of architectural history was demolished in 1960, shortly after the new library building was erected in 1958. The University of Michigan–Flint campus now sprawls across the area where the Carnegie library once stood.

In January 2016, reference librarian Vera Anderson published an article in the library's newsletter about her first encounter with the library's ghost, which happened decades before. Grant told Anderson about the resident spook, but she had remained skeptical until one night while working alone in the dark building. A loud bang occurred outside her office, and she investigated and found a large tome on the floor.

> *But the book hadn't merely fallen off the shelf, a near impossibility as the shelves were both deep and strong—and the substantial book had been placed well back from the edge. No. It hadn't simply fallen off the shelf.*

It had flown out into the center of the room, landing a good five feet from the shelf. It had landed on its spine—and had flown open. Not just open; the pages were turning, as if blown by a stiff wind (or flipped by unseen fingers?). Had there been a breeze, perhaps the hair on the back of my neck would not have risen.

She relayed the story to Grant the next day, and he smiled and said she had met the resident researcher.

Since Grant's passing, Vera wonders if he visits the library in spirit form, perhaps to hang out with the spooky page flipper and work on a project together.

3

MURDER LEAVES A MARK

WESTWOOD PARTY SHOPPE (FLINT)

When I was young I was terrified of the shadowy corner store by my house. It sat there—dark and boarded up, closed for a good decade or so. The energy emanating from it terrified me. I always wished my mom would take a different route driving home at night. One night when we driving by it, I told my mom how much it spooked me. She told me it spooked her too and for good reason. The man who owned it had been killed during a robbery and stuffed in the freezer. When the store finally opened back up, when I was around ten or eleven years old, I did not want to go in it, ever, but they were the only store that always had the new bubble gum flavors—which was a big deal to me in the '80s. So I would run into the store, get my gum and never, ever go near the coolers. I always felt like the ghost of the murdered man was in there, waiting for me.

On the evening of January 24, 1976, Francis A. Plourde, age fifty-eight, was working in his store, Westwood Party Shoppe, at the corner of Pierson and Linden Roads in Mt. Morris Township when a robbery occurred around eight o'clock.

Francis was shot in the head and stuffed in the cooler. His body was found by Albert D. Hanner of Flushing, who stopped at the store around 9:00 p.m. Plourde was still alive at the time and was rushed to McLaren General Hospital, where he died around 2:00 a.m. An undetermined amount of money was taken from the register; state police believe it was less than one hundred dollars.

At some point during the robbery, Katherine Rohner, age forty-five, was taken hostage. No one knows if she interrupted the robbery, was already in the store when the robbery occurred or bumped into the robber as he ran out of the store, because Rohner's car was found outside the store with a bag of groceries in it. Rohner's body was found on Monday, January 26, when a fifth-grade boy was playing during recess at the John R. Rice Baptist Academies on Coldwater Road about two miles from the robbery location. He spotted a boot protruding from a snowdrift near a classroom window. He told his teacher about it, and she told him to grab the boot. When he tried to get the boot, he realized it was attached to something; the boy thought at first it was a mannequin. Poor kid, it was the body of Katherine Rohner buried in the snow. Rohner had been fatally shot in the head, just like Plourde. So why kidnap her? An autopsy later revealed that she had been raped.

State police had no leads until two convicts in the Genesee County Jail accused each other of the crime. Clarence J. Green accused Charles Mason Ewing of the murders. Green tied Ewing to three other crimes as well. During the preliminary hearing, Green testified under oath that he knew Ewing was responsible because he was there and witnessed the murder of Plourde and the abduction, rape and murder of Rohner. Green described in detail what happened but said he had no part in the murder or rape. He was a thief, not a killer. Ewing then accused Green of the crime, saying that Green confessed the party store murder-rape to him in early 1976. He also connected Green to the robbery and rape of a sixteen-year-old at a Kentucky Fried Chicken on Pierson Road. Green was a suspect in the crime, but the victim could not identify him.

The Baptist Academy is now Northridge Academy, and the Westwood Party Shoppe is now called The Works.

Turns out Roxanne isn't the only one to be spooked by the party store: when discussing the location with folks online, she discovered that many people who live or have lived in the area have avoided The Works because of "bad vibes." They always stop at a different store, even though The Works is conveniently located right on the corner. One Facebook reader, who wished to remain anonymous, said that they always get the chills and feel like someone is watching them when they shopped at The Works. Another contributor, who also wished to remain anonymous, had a few encounters at The Works that spooked her so bad she refuses to go back. She said that one time she stopped in late at night to grab a six-pack of beer on her way to a party. She was the only shopper in the store. While standing in front of the cooler deciding what to purchase, she felt arms wrap around her and pull. She stumbled and lost her balance. Freaked out, she whipped around to confront her assailant, but no one was there. She convinced herself she imagined it because she was tired. She grabbed some beer, paid and left. Her next visit to the store was similar, late at night, empty store—this time, while perusing the shelves, she felt a hand go over her mouth and an arm encircle her waist. No one was there. She was done. Terrified, she left without purchasing anything and has never returned. She had no previous knowledge of the murder that happened there.

Many paranormal investigators believe when something traumatic happens in a location, dark energy can remain and those sensitive to it will avoid the spot. Murder leaves a mark, far beyond bloodstains on the floor. Murder stains the metaphysical fabric of a location. Ghosts may or may not roam the premises of the store, but the location remains haunted by the murder that occurred decades ago.

4

CROSSROADS VILLAGE AND HUCKLEBERRY RAILROAD (FLINT)

enesee County has a special treasure tucked away just outside Flint—Crossroads Village and Huckleberry Railroad. When you walk into the village, you are transported through time. The buildings are all from the mid- to late 1800s, the oldest dating back to 1836. They were all carefully moved, rebuilt and restored on land that was once a strawberry farm. Now they are showcased with furniture and décor from 1860 to 1880; some even have items from the original owners, including photos, wedding dresses, teacups and musical instruments.

Crossroads Village is a location where the past collides with the present. Modern-day tourists roam the village, enjoying a glimpse of the past, seeing how people lived in the late 1800s, while they never have to give up their modern conveniences like cellphones or WiFi. The village is a liminal space, stuck in the past while simultaneously existing in the present.

With buildings and train cars so old it's hard to imagine there isn't a ghost or two attached to them, but have no fear, the stories whispered about the ghosts of Crossroads aren't scary. It seems several residents just continue to linger in the places where they lived and died. Some like to play pranks, while others are just shadows of the past, time slips showcasing an era gone by. Echoes of happiness and laughter linger, mixing and mingling with voices of the past.

Crossroads Village opened on July 4, 1976, but the preservation of several of the structures started in 1967, when the historic buildings were

The Huckleberry Railroad

Huckleberry Railroad postcard. *Author collection.*

going to be demolished to make way for the I-475 freeway. Ken Smithee moved them to their current location. At that time, there was no plan other than to keep them safe.

In December 1968, a proposal to save the old buildings and reassemble them as a museum was presented to the Genesee County Board of Commissioners by John West and Stanley Mahaffy. The Genesee County Parks and Recreation Commission, Genesee County Historical Society, Flint Beautification Commission, Flint Housing Commission, the Mallory Charitable Trust, the C.S. Mott Foundation and many others were engaged in the project.

In June 1969, the Buzzell House and Judge Wisner's carriage house were the first to be rescued; they were soon followed by the Eldridge House (1860s). The Genesee County Parks and Recreation Commission granted $20,000 to move the first two buildings to land donated by the C.S. Mott Foundation.

During the summer of 1973, the Genesee County Board of Supervisors provided funding to begin their bicentennial project; the plan was approved in 1974. In the fall of 1974, the Clayton Town Hall and the Davison Train Depot were moved to the site. In 1975, the Flint Township Hall, the Atlas Grist Mill (built by Judge Norman Davison in 1836), the

Fox House, the Masters Cider Mill and the Stanley School House (1883) were moved to Crossroads.

The Coldwater Road Chapel (1889) was added in 1977. In 1978, the first floor of the Horton-Colwell Opera House opened at Crossroads. The entire structure was moved and rebuilt brick by brick from its original location in Fenton. In 1979, the Print Shop was moved to the village. In 1980, the second-floor opera house of the Horton-Colwell building was completed. While in Fenton, this opera house boasted such acts as General Tom Thumb and singer Lillie Langtry. In 1981, the Attica Hotel (1870s) was moved from Lake Pleasant Road in Lapeer County to the Village. In 1983, the 1912 Charles W. Parker Carousel was moved to Crossroads. The beautiful hand-carved wooden horses reside next to Parker's Superior Wheel, which was built in 1910 and arrived at Crossroads in 1991. In 1988, the Fowler Barber Shop moved into the village. In 1990, the Millstreet Warehouse was added to resemble a turn-of-the-century warehouse to offer food service and space for special events. Other buildings that arrived in the 1990s were the Fenton Barn, also known as the Broom Barn, and the Salter Log Home (1840). In 1992, the Venetian Swings were added to the collection of vintage rides. The *Genesee Belle*, a Mark Twain–era riverboat replica, was added in 1995 as an attraction. The latest addition is the Mason Tavern (1850), which was moved from Grand Blanc.

The main attraction of Crossroads Village is the Huckleberry Railroad. It was a huge task to track down all the equipment, train cars and steam engines to assemble the historically accurate train. The railroad takes visitors on a forty-minute journey with an authentic Baldwin steam locomotive. During the ride, visitors get to see the shores of Mott Lake, part of the historic Pere Marquette roadbed and the heart of Crossroads Village. The Huckleberry Railroad was once a real freight line, a subsidiary of the Pere Marquette established in 1857. It was officially known as the Flint Pere Marquette Railroad Company. According to the park's website, "The Huckleberry Railroad was named because it ran so slow, a person could jump off the train, pick a few huckleberries, and jump back on the train with minimum effort."

A man spotted a ghostly train car crossing Bray Road one night after he left Crossroads Village. While reports of other ghost train sightings or even deaths on the train have not been found, there was a death by train on the Pere Marquette line in June 1901. Major George W. Buckingham and his daughter Anna, of Flint, along with their houseguests Mrs. Applegate and Mrs. Humphrey of Adrian, were killed instantly when their carriage was

Huckleberry Railroad caboose. *Photo by Roxanne Rhoads.*

struck by a train going at least fifty miles per hour. The bodies were loaded into the train and taken to the Pere Marquette Depot, where the bodies were stored in the baggage area until they could be taken to the undertaker.

The Davison Train Depot was a flag stop along the Grand Trunk Railroad line in Davison, Michigan. When it was restored in 1974 at Crossroads Village, it was painted its original colors. The depot is said to be haunted by a former security guard who hanged himself in his office. Now he likes to play pranks on the current guards by rustling paperwork, moving things around and setting off alarms all over the village. There are rumors but no records of a suicidal security guard; however, there were numerous deaths at and near the Davison depot railroad tracks. In March 1913, eighty-year-old Civil War veteran James Roberts was killed right by the Davison Depot. The man, whose hearing was impaired, was sitting on the tracks and didn't hear the train coming. He tried to get up when he realized there was a train, but it was too late. In May 1913, teamster Paul Ward and his horses were struck by a westbound passenger train at the depot crossing. The carriage, horses and driver were thrown over two hundred yards.

Davison Train Depot at Crossroads. *Photo by Roxanne Rhoads.*

Numerous former employees at Crossroads have experienced the feeling of eyes watching them wherever they go in the village. One said, "You're never alone, even when the buildings are empty."

Several who have worked in the Stanley School House, built in 1883, reported the sounds of children running and laughing though no children were present. The spirit of a young boy tries to interact with the workers, flickering lights and casting strange shadows. Imagine all the children that have passed through the building while it was in operation from 1883 to 1963. The sounds are probably just echoes through time, nothing sinister to worry about. The schoolhouse still teaches children today through the Stanley School House program in which local schools can bring in students to be taught in an authentic one-room schoolhouse, using teaching styles and materials from the 1800s. Students, chaperones and teachers are encouraged to dress in clothing typical of the 1800s.

Rumors say that the Atlas Grist Mill's attic contains the lingering spirit of a woman. She is allegedly a former mill worker's wife who died in the mill. One former employee used to see her wandering around a window at the top of the stairs.

Stanley School House. *Photo by Roxanne Rhoads.*

Atlas Grist Mill. *Photo by Roxanne Rhoads.*

The opera house has a story involving a light tech who likes to play pranks on workers. Many people have experienced strange things in the opera house like hearing the voice of a woman echoing in the darkness. The ghostly scent of lilacs can sometimes be detected even though no source for the flowery aroma has ever been found.

Across the street, at the Attica Hotel, a woman in white is often spotted on the balcony. The Attica Hotel was built by lumber baron William Williams. Sources have conflicting dates about the build year—some say 1850–58, others note it was built in the 1870s. Around 1881, the building became the Schirmer House. Over the years, it was a post office, an apartment building, multiple stores and, of course, an elegant hotel with a second-floor ballroom that opened onto the balcony. Attica residents loved to regale each other with tales of ballroom brawls and people going over the balcony. The hotel survived a fire in the early 1900s.

The George H. Durand Home and Law Office is rumored to be haunted by a former owner who hanged themselves on the upper level. No one will work in the building alone at night, and it is often open but not staffed because so many employees are creeped out by the eerie feeling in the building. One former employee felt whatever lurked in the old law office was sinister and wanted nothing to do with it. This 1850s home office, originally located on Davison Road in Burton Township, is named after the first president of the Genesee Bar Association, George Harman Durand, who practiced law in

George H. Durand Home and Law Office. *Photo by Roxanne Rhoads.*

Mason Tavern Inn. *Photo by Roxanne Rhoads.*

Flint, Michigan, where he was also a member of the Board of Education in the 1860s. He was mayor of Flint in 1873 and 1874. In 1874, he was elected as a Democrat to Congress and served from 1875 to 1877. After serving in Congress, he resumed his law practice and was appointed justice of the Michigan Supreme Court in 1892. He passed away in Flint in 1903 and is buried in Glenwood Cemetery. The Michigan community of Durand was named after him.

Daniel Mason built the Mason Tavern Inn around 1850. It was a popular stagecoach stop along the route of the Flint and Fentonville Plank Road Company. From 1853 to 1871, the Mundy Township post office was also housed there. In 1879, Mason sold the property and moved to Flint, where he died in 1880. The year the Mason Tavern was added to Crossroads Village, a worker passing out candy during the Ghosts and Goodies event continually felt someone tugging at her hair and her cloak though no one was ever there. Someone from beyond really wanted her attention.

There have been a couple of strange experiences at the Fox House. Jackson Fox built the house in 1876, and he resided in the beautiful home until he died in 1899. The house stood at the corner of Carpenter and Branch Roads until 1975, when it was donated to Crossroads Village. Today, it contains photos of Jackson; his wife, Adeline; and their ten children, along

Fox House. *Photo by Roxanne Rhoads.*

Buzzell House. *Photo by Roxanne Rhoads.*

with many items the family-owned. Numerous people have reported feeling the strong spirit presence of a man in the house, but one former Crossroads employee personally felt someone come up behind her and wrap one arm around her waist while the other touched her hair. She often heard footsteps upstairs even though she knew she was alone in the house.

In 1854, carpenter John Buzzell built a home for his family where he and his wife, Kathryn, lived with their three sons. The Buzzell House was one of the first buildings moved to the land that would eventually become Crossroads Village. At the time of its relocation, it was the oldest standing wooden structure in Flint. The Buzzell House is rumored to be active with spirits. Two former employees have sensed spirits there at night. A former maintenance man felt like there was a kindly spirit on the second floor encouraging him to go upstairs.

None of the claims of accidental deaths or suicides in the Crossroads buildings have been substantiated, though multiple people who worked at Crossroads swear a security guard in the 1980s hanged himself somewhere on the property.

5

SEX, LIES AND A JUNKYARD MURDER (CLIO)

Hulks of twisted, rusted, abandoned steel reside in a yard full of discarded parts and pieces of vehicles, long-forgotten memories of times gone by. How many vehicles end up in a junkyard because of a fatal car accident? How many vehicles get sent to the scrap yard after their owners were found dead inside? With all the trauma and despair attached to some of these forgotten remnants of the past, it's not hard to believe specters lurk among the wreckage.

One Genesee County junkyard has multiple tales of ghostly sightings and a high-profile murder attached to it. The salvage yard is located near Auto City Speedway race track in Clio, Michigan. The murder was covered in the book *Fatal Error* by Mark Morris and a Lifetime movie, *Fatal Desire*, featuring Anne Heche and Eric Roberts in the lead roles. It was also featured on *Forensic Files* season 19, episode 4, "Web of Seduction." The narrator said the story "had everything: sex, lies and a video tape."

On November 8, 1999, Chuck Miller received a frantic phone call from his sister-in-law. His brother Bruce was missing. He wasn't answering his phone at work and hadn't come home for dinner. Chuck went to look for him. Bruce Miller was found on the floor of his office at B&D Auto Parts and Salvage located on North Saginaw Road. He had been shot in the chest. The phone receiver was on the floor next to him. The $2,000 he normally kept on him to make change for customers was missing, so at first, it was assumed to be a robbery.

But the crime scene was too clean.

Six months before the murder, forty-eight-year-old Bruce had married twenty-eight-year-old Sharee Kitley. He was her third husband and was planning to adopt her three children. By all accounts, this hardworking man who was employed at General Motors and owned a junkyard was a great guy. So who would want him dead? The spouse is always considered first, but friends and family all said the marriage between Bruce and Sharee was a happy one.

Sharee had been home all day with her children and was not considered a suspect, but she had an idea of who was. She tried to blame the murder on her ex-boyfriend John Hutchinson, whose brother Harold worked at the junkyard. She said John and Bruce argued a lot and that Hutchinson stole from the junkyard. John Hutchinson had no alibi for the time of the murder and failed a polygraph test—he even collapsed during it. But the police could find no evidence to connect him to the murder. An autopsy revealed Bruce was killed with a 20-gauge shotgun.

It took a death seven hundred miles away in Kansas City, Missouri, for the detectives to finally catch a real break in the case. Former homicide detective Jerry Cassaday was found dead with a gun in his hand and a Bible on his lap. Divorce papers were found on his desk. In a trash can outside his home, police found a videotape marked "For Jerry's eyes only." The video was a homemade tape of a woman dancing seductively. His friends said the video was of Jerry's girlfriend, who lived in Flint, Michigan, and was named Sharee.

Sharee was brought into police headquarters for questioning; while there, she claimed she didn't know who Jerry Cassaday was. When confronted with the videotape, she changed her story, confessing that she knew him but he was crazy. She finally admitted she met him in a computer chatroom. Sharee and Jerry's computers were confiscated by forensics. This was one of the first cases in which computer forensics and internet data were used to help prosecute a crime. The trial was billed as the internet's first murder case and was covered by Court TV. The case was later dubbed the Instant Message Murder.

The forensics team found AOL instant message chats in which Sharee and Jerry discussed murder. Sharee gave Jerry detailed instructions on where to find Bruce, what door to enter, what to take. She guided him through everything step by step. Sharee denied everything, claiming the messages were forged. AOL confirmed that it was a possibility. Court orders forced AOL to release details about Sharee and Jerry's activity, confirming they were both logged into their accounts on the same day and time for the exact length of time as the instant message. This proved the message was not forged. Another damning piece of evidence was found in Sharee's computer desk—the name John P Occonnor and a phone number written in her handwriting on an envelope. This name had been mentioned in the AOL Instant Message by Jerry; Sharee should contact him if anything happened to Jerry. The name was misspelled and the phone number wrong in both the message and Sharee's handwritten note. This confirmed she wrote it down directly from the AOL instant message.

Sharee and Jerry met in an AOL chatroom, eventually meeting in person and becoming lovers; when they were not together, she would send him erotic photos and videos. According to Oxygen's *Snapped*, Sharee and a friend went on a vacation to Reno in July 1999, where she and Jerry met in person. At the time, he was working as a pit boss in a Reno casino. Jerry told his co-worker and friend Carol Slaughter that Sharee would "do absolutely anything in the bedroom."

At one point, Sharee claimed to be pregnant with Jerry's twins. He had no idea she'd had a tubal ligation years earlier. She used the charade to control him. She had a plan. Bait consisted of a photo of a positive pregnancy test that was her friend's and a photo of a sonogram from one of her previous pregnancies—these lured him in. Then she set the trap by telling Jerry that Bruce was a drug dealer, a member of the mafia and a wife beater. Finally, Sharee told Jerry that Bruce beat her so bad she miscarried the twins, sending him photos of her bruised body that she faked with makeup.

Jerry took the bait and decided to ride in like a white knight and save the princess from her evil captor. They made plans to get rid of Bruce via AOL instant messaging. Sharee kept Bruce distracted on the phone while Jerry went in and shot him. Phone records confirmed this. Jerry's experience as a homicide detective helped him clean up the scene and leave no evidence behind.

A few weeks after the murder, Sharee ghosted Jerry: she stopped taking his calls and no longer messaged him. She just dropped him. Grief-stricken and filled with despair over his actions, he took his own life. In a suicide note left for his parents, Jerry confessed to the murder. Sadly, he had bought most of Sharee's lies. He honestly believed Bruce had beaten her and killed his unborn children, but he did realize that he had been duped and that Sharee just wanted money without the burden of a husband. He confessed she helped plan everything and had proof. The proof was a briefcase full of copies of the instant messages and emails implicating Sharee in the murder. A dead man's confession proved Sharee's guilt.

Sharee was arrested in February 2000 and held without bail until her trial in December. Her trial began on December 12, 2000. She continually denied any involvement, claiming that she was innocent and the instant messages were forged. On December 22, after two days of jury deliberation, she was found guilty of all charges. On January 29, 2001, Genesee County Circuit Court judge Judith A. Fullerton sentenced Sharee Miller to life in prison for the conspiracy to commit murder and fifty-four to eighty-one years for second-degree murder.

In August 2008, a federal court judge overturned her conviction and ordered that she receive a new trial because the judge decided that the suicide note from Cassaday should never have been admitted into court and seen by the jurors because Cassaday was dead and could not be cross-examined. Sharee Miller was released from prison. She was arraigned again on July 22, 2009, on charges of second-degree murder and conspiracy to commit premeditated first-degree murder. On July 29, 2009, Sharee was released from the Genesee County Jail on a $100,000 recognizance bond until her new trial began. The case went through the U.S Court of Appeals and the U.S. Supreme Court for years until February 2014, when the court finally decided the suicide note was admissible and the court reinstated Miller's original convictions and sentences.

In April 2016, over sixteen years after the murder, after almost seventeen years of claiming to be innocent, Sharee Miller sent a four-page typed letter to Judge Judith Fullerton and admitted to her role in her husband's death.

> *I manipulated a man into killing another man....*
> *Judge Fullerton, I did it. Almost the way the prosecutor said I did....*
> *I knew it was going to happen and I allowed it. I allowed a man to kill another man based on my lies and manipulation.*

Sharee Miller's attorney, David Nickola, said the case could have turned out differently if his client had been truthful from the beginning. A plea agreement was offered before the trial, and she could have served a lesser sentence.

For decades, this case fascinated residents of Genesee County. Now the site of the murder is rumored to be haunted. John Robinson, the author of *Haunted Michigan*, featured the junkyard in his column at 99.1 WFMK. Motorists who drive by at night have reported hearing screams coming from the property, long after the place had closed. Local police have received numerous calls from motorists who have claimed to see human figures standing by the road as if they were seeking some kind of assistance. When the motorists stopped, the figures suddenly disappeared. One police report claims a motorist thought he hit someone standing by the road, but when he stopped, there was no one there and no damage was done to his vehicle.

Roxanne spoke with Linda Bolduc, whose ex-husband, Jerry Bolduc Sr., purchased the salvage yard after Bruce Miller's murder. There was a lot of interest in the location from paranormal researchers. One research team found quite a bit of evidence pointing to paranormal activity and multiple spirits at the site. Linda said whenever a door would open by itself (which happened quite often), they would just say, "Come on in, Bruce." They welcomed their junkyard ghost. Linda was adamant that the ghostly activity was never sinister and their junkyard spirit was simply a good guy who married a bad woman and paid for that mistake with his life.

A current employee at the location often hears banging outside after dark; he'll go to check it out but can never find a source for the noise. The office often has unexplained cold spots. Many think the spirit of Bruce Miller is still lingering in his office and roaming around his junkyard. But what about the other strange sightings? Did the violence of Bruce's murder awaken spirits attached to abandoned vehicles?

6

THE BRENT ESTATE AND DOROTHY SCHNEIDER (FLUSHING)

The city of Flushing is a picturesque area with a small-town feel, and residents work hard to keep it that way. Crime and scandal are often swept under the rug and never make headlines in the local news unless they are so heinous they can't be ignored. Ghost stories are another thing Flushing likes to keep under wraps. There are faint whispers about ghosts at Goggins Hall. There's a story about a ghost girl at the old junior high school building, which is now the Early Childhood Center (ECC). It is rumored to be haunted by a girl who fell to her death from one of the upper-story windows. The basement of the ECC is so eerie no one likes to go down there. Then there's the subdivision dubbed "The Reservation" because most of the streets have Native American names—there are quite a few whispered rumors about spirit-filled houses where suicides and murders have taken place, but when you try to find any details or get more than whispers, no one wants to talk.

There is one story people are more than happy to talk about. For almost two centuries, the Flushing area has been fascinated by tales of the wealthy Brent family who came from Virginia with a wife thought to be Spanish royalty. Numerous newspaper articles were published about them well into the late twentieth century. Why? Because their family and the large amount of land they owned is connected to numerous tales of murder, mystery and ghosts.

Thomas Ludwell Lee Brent was the son of a Virginian senator and traveled across Europe as a young man. He built up quite a reputation and fortune along the way. While in Spain, he fell in love and married Francesca—rumors say she was Spanish royalty. Brent took his new bride home to Washington, D.C., but she was never happy there. Francesca confided to the first lady, Dolley Madison, that she was homesick.

In 1814, President Madison appointed Brent the secretary of U.S. legation in Madrid. In 1822, President Monroe appointed him secretary of the legation at Lisbon. From 1824 to 1834, Brent was the chargé d'affaires to Portugal. As a diplomat, he regularly sent communications to the U.S. State Department. Diplomatic relations between the United States and Portugal were severed in 1834, so Brent returned home to Virginia with his wife and two children, only to be disowned by his father due to religious differences.

Eventually, Brent headed north with his wife and two children and arrived in the Flushing area around 1835–36. There he purchased an astounding amount of land, over seventy thousand acres. He intended to build a lumber empire.

Brent promptly built a dam across the Flint River in Section 3 and erected a sawmill. The dam was washed away in 1837 by a freshet, and the sawmill was ruined. A new dam and mill were built. This mill was set farther away from the river but was never large enough to be practical.

Large areas of the forest were cleared for farmland and Brent's beautiful home. The Brents chose a spot about four miles north of present-day Flushing on a U-bend of the Flint River. First, a log cabin was built, followed by a grand Colonial-style mansion they named Rosemont. It is said that the Brent household was not a happy one. The couple often fought, and the family lived under a sad and mysterious shroud. Thomas died in 1845 before Rosemont was completed. It is said his coffin had to be lowered out of an upstairs window because the winding staircase was too fancy to accommodate it being taken down.

Thomas Brent had been a successful diplomat, but he was a terrible businessman. He had expended his capital to the point where he had no reserve to pay taxes. Pieces of his land were sold off at discounted prices and traded to pay debts.

Francesca and the children continued building their new home in grand style. It had a music room with the first piano in Genesee County. The house was furnished with costly furniture trucked in from Detroit. Francesca Brent had a complete wardrobe of formal dresses. The Brents entertained in top style. While the money lasted, the Brents lived grandly in the style of the Virginia planter aristocracy. Many other Flushing-area settlers made their fortunes working on Brent's farms. Eventually, the Brent estate consisted of just three to six hundred acres. It is thought that this area is what became known as Brent Creek, a small community within Flushing Township on Mt. Morris Road between Nichols Road and Seymour Road.

The widow and her children were terrible at handling the finances, even more so than Thomas. Mrs. Brent was an easy mark for the land grabbers. The debts and losses wore on her. Francesca's physical and mental health declined. Rumors swirled that Thomas Brent's ghost haunted the home, calling out for his wife.

Brent's daughter Charlotte fell in love with a married farmer, Devillo Palmer, and got pregnant. Palmer's wife died of mysterious circumstances. Palmer was tried but not convicted due to a lack of evidence.

Charlotte's mother did not approve of the couple. Just six months after they married on October 19, 1858, Francesca died of arsenic poisoning. Charlotte and her brother Henry Brent were arrested and indicted for their mother's murder but never put on trial. Charlotte's husband, Devillo, was the chief suspect in the murder, but he conveniently disappeared before he could be arrested. Charlotte and Henry were released in June 1859 due to a lack of evidence and testimony.

Charlotte left the area with her son, and it is thought that Henry J. Brent joined the Civil War and was never heard from again. But a letter written by Henry to Charlotte on November 24, 1861, appeared in a New York newspaper, *The Sun and the Erie County Independent*, in September 1959. It detailed a return trip home from Buffalo, New York. The letter shows he returned to Michigan in 1861, docking in Detroit, and then mentions "going home" to Charlotte. So even though they left Flushing, they didn't leave Michigan at first. Vital records indicate that Henry and Charlotte lived in Buffalo, New York, in 1869. Charlotte never remarried. Henry never married or had children. Charlotte passed away in New York in 1890, and Henry Lee Brent died on May 13, 1908. Henry's obituary indicated that he reinvented himself in Buffalo as an artist, musician and linguist. Charlotte and Devillo's son, Ralph Henry Palmer, served in the military during the Spanish-American War. He married and had two daughters; one daughter had two sons, but neither of them had any children. There are no records of what happened to Devillo Palmer.

Francesca and Thomas were buried in unmarked graves in Glenwood Cemetery until 1997, when documents were found detailing the grave plot purchased by Henry and Charlotte for their parents. The Montrose Historical Society purchased a twelve-by-twenty-four-inch headstone and placed it on their grave 151 years after Thomas Brent died.

Rosemont was known as Flushing's most haunted house for years; several former residents will attest to that. Legend says that on bright moonlit nights, you can see Thomas wandering along the river. Some have claimed to see both Thomas and Francesca wandering in the moonlight.

Carol Swanson and her family lived in the mansion from 1947 to 1960. She told the *Flint Journal* that there were many strange happenings. Things would move though no human hands ever touched them.

Some people claim that the ghost of Thomas Brent constantly roamed the mansion. They could hear him stomp up and down the stairs looking for Francesca.

For about sixty years, the estate was owned by the Bishops, a prominent family of Flint. They restored the buildings and developed the orchards. In 1966, the land was split; the new owner kept a piece to raise Arabian horses, and Rosemont, then known as Brentwood Manor and Barcelonia, was demolished to make way for a subdivision.

The legacy Brent leaves behind is Brent's Creek in Flushing, Brent Run in Montrose, and the Brentwood Farms subdivision in Flushing township— and a history full of murder, mystery and ghosts on the lands that once belonged to the Brent family.

On an episode of *The Dead Files* titled "Triggered" (season 9, episode 1, first aired in February 2018), hosts Amy Allan and Steve Di Schiavi investigate a house that is on the land the Brents originally owned.

After moving into the home, the new residents underwent emotional changes and started suffering from depression. Then physical attacks from unseen entities started. There were odd voices, footsteps and shadow figures. The health of the residents was greatly affected. The children would often see a shadowy man with facial hair in a top hat.

Amy sensed an influence that pushed males to violence and a female spirit upstairs who was worried about the children being in danger. Amy also sensed two violent males.

Steve uncovered a violent past tied to the Brent land that included the murder of Charlotte Brent's husband Devillo Palmer's first wife. Most interesting was the child spirit Amy sensed: a little ghost girl running around in old-fashioned attire. She's outside, something happens to her, then she's dead. The little ghost girl showed Amy an evil entity seen as a bubbling tar monster.

Amy and Steve thought the ghost girl might be Palmer's murdered child, but historical records show only that he was charged with his wife's murder. There is no record of a child, though old newspaper articles mention that long after the Brents were gone, the skeletal remains of a woman and child were found along the path to the Brent home.

Dorothy Schneider.
Author collection.

Another possibility is that the ghost girl could be Dorothy Schneider. Amy's description of the spirit eerily matches newspaper photos of little Dorothy.

On January 12, 1928, five-year-old Dorothy, daughter of Kenneth and Mabel Schneider, was walking home from Kindergarten on Dixie Highway in Mt. Morris. Her mother, Mabel, was looking out the window, watching for her daughter. She spotted a car stop a couple of blocks away and saw the door open and close, but the view was obstructed by trees and her infant son, Kenneth, started crying and distracted her. Minutes ticked by, and Dorothy did not arrive home.

By noon, Mabel had become frantic and called the school, learning that Dorothy had left at her usual time. She then took her son to a neighbor and frantically ran to the village police department and spoke with Deputy Sheriff Harry D. Gleason. Gleason questioned locals and discovered that a blue Dodge had filled up at the pump of Sid Hodges's gas station right after Dorothy had walked by.

Gleason followed vehicle tracks through muddy roads and fields to the wooded banks of Brent Creek. Caught on an elderberry bush were a child's hat, sweater and jacket. Three hours had passed since Dorothy was kidnapped. He knew that if she had been thrown into the frigid creek, the poor little girl was beyond help.

Gleason went searching for a phone at the local farm of Archie Bacon. He had to call in reinforcements to help search for Dorothy. Archie Bacon was horrified at the news: "My God I helped that devil get out the mud hole with his car," he cried. "About noon I saw a man carrying a bundle across the fields. Two hours later this fellow with the blue Dodge came to the house on foot and asked me to help get the car out of that hole. I did and he drove off toward Clio Road on the gravel." He then gave Gleason a description of the man, saying he was about fifty years old, 190 pounds and walked with a stoop.

Darkness was falling when the search came to a horrific conclusion. Deputy Fred Dormire plunged into the icy water and searched along the bottom of the muddy creek until he suddenly stopped a few yards from the elderberry bush. He stood up carrying the naked, mutilated body of little Dorothy. The poor child had been brutally beaten, raped and viciously shredded.

Location where Dorothy Schneider's body was found. *Author collection*.

The Sunday following the murder, Harold Lotridge was installed as deacon, succeeding Adolph Hotelling, at the Church of Christ in Owosso, thirty miles from Mt. Morris. That night, he suffered a heart attack and dreamed of murder.

Almost two decades later, a *Detroit Free Press* article recounted the tale of the "Strange Case of the Nightmare That Revealed a Child-Murderer": "Harold Lotridge, Owosso carpenter and lay leader of the Church of Christ, had been a witness to the hideous ravishment and butchery of a little girl. He had seen the blood, the knife, the murderer's contorted face. Worse still, he had recognized the monster as a man long his friend and fellow worker and churchman."

The man was none other than Adolph Hotelling, the elder whom Lotridge had just replaced as deacon. Lotridge told his father about the dream the next day and asked whether he should turn in his church elder. Another church member overheard the conversation, believed that Lotridge had actually witnessed the horrible event, and drove quickly to Flint to tell the police. He returned to the church accompanied by Deputies Mark Pailthorpe, Henry Munger and Thomas Kelley. The officers questioned the young deacon and discovered he didn't witness the crime but dreamed about it.

"Of all the nutty tips that we've investigated so far, this one takes the prize," one deputy chuckled. "The deacon sees an elder of his church killing a child in a dream phooey."

Even though they thought it to be farfetched, they went to Hotelling's home. While questioning him, Deputy Pailthorpe accidentally scraped Hotelling's black Dodge, revealing the robin's egg blue paint underneath. When the deputies questioned Hotelling's wife, they discovered he repainted it the day after Dorothy's murder. They arrested him. On the drive to Flint, Hotelling went nuts, whipped out a knife and tried to slice his own throat. The knife contained pieces of fabric matching those cut from Dorothy and was covered in dried blood. At the station, Archie Bacon confirmed Hotelling's identity as the man he helped free the Dodge from a mud hole. After his identification, Hotelling confessed to the murder and threw himself on the ground screaming that the devil made him do it.

Judging by maps and old newspaper clippings, it looks like Dorothy's body was found in Brent Creek on land that once was part of the Brent Estate.

Many people who have hiked through wooded areas along Brent's Creek have reported hearing a child's laughter, though there is never a child found in the area.

Dorothy Schneider funeral. *Author collection.*

Nicole B., a Flushing resident who lives on Coldwater Road, said she hears laughter and two little girls talking when no one is around. Sometimes it is in her barn, sometimes in the backyard. Brent Creek runs through her property. She also reported seeing shadow people and the ghostly figure of a man, similar to the reports from the house on the *Dead Files*. Is little Dorothy's spirit lingering in the area where she was killed?

Little Dorothy is buried in Sunset Hills Cemetery, a Flint hot spot of ghostly activity and urban legend. The story of the cemetery is covered in chapter 10 of *Haunted Flint*.

Nearby on McKinley Road is the Flushing Township Nature Park, which abuts the Brentwood Farms subdivision. The land was originally set aside to be part of the subdivision along the Flint River, but in 1992, it was suggested that it become a nature park. These areas were part of the original Brent Estate. The park is thick with the spirits of Native Americans. The spirits of the Sauk who were slaughtered by the Ojibwa are doomed to roam the land for all eternity, or so infers author Curtis J. Scott, who grew up on the land that is now the Flushing Township Nature Park. On his Facebook page, he tells the stories of his haunted life. He details his numerous encounters with Native American spirits, unfortunate victims of the notorious Purple Gang, several people who drowned in the Flint River and a mysterious ghostly carriage thought to be the Brent's that has been seen as far north as the Montrose Orchard but is more often seen blasting down Nashua Trail and over the Flint River. Curtis gives details on the many encounters he has had with the spirits of Thomas and Francesca Brent, the latter of whom tended to appear to him as a beautiful young teenager instead of the old woman she was when she died. Curtis even mentions an English man dubbed the Demon of McKinley Road who has purportedly killed numerous women by causing them to wreck their cars along a dangerous curve on McKinley Road. Many residents in Brentwood Farms and along McKinley Road have dealt with spirits and strange occurrences, and many have mentioned seeing the spirits of Native Americans. Some even claim to have Native burial mounds on their land.

For centuries, people have whispered that the murdered Sauk cursed the land they perished on. Many who have lived on the land once belonging to the Sauk have suffered—the Ojibwa, the Brents, numerous people who died in car accidents and several children who were hit by cars. There is something sinister about the area that once belonged to the Brents and the places that hold their name. This land doesn't like to give up its dead. Spirits continue to wander the woods and roadways long after their bodies are gone.

7

MARY CRAPO SCHOOL
(SWARTZ CREEK)

Shadow figures, voices in empty rooms, items that moved by themselves—the Mary Crapo School left plenty of former students and staff with spooky memories of their time in the building.

Henry H. Crapo was Michigan's fourteenth governor. He built the railroad from Flint to Holly to expand lumber markets. When he died in 1869, his farm in Gaines Township was passed to his only son William, who was a lawyer in Massachusetts. In 1876, the expansion of the railroad was set to go right through the family farm. William Crapo's skillful negotiations saved the farm, and he obtained the right to use the railroad's drainage ditches and had a private side track built. The track offered visitors a private depot on the property and allowed cattle and produce to be shipped directly to and from the farm. It was the only farm in North America to have a private train depot. The Crapo family was instrumental in the development of the Miller settlement and Swartz Creek. Eventually, parts of the land were donated for the St. Mary's Cemetery and the Mary Crapo School.

In addition to the donation of the land, S.T. Crapo donated $40,000 for the construction of the school that was to be named after Henry H. Crapo's wife, Mary. The school opened in 1929 and housed kindergarten through twelfth grade. The first graduating class of 1930 featured four students. Eventually, new schools were built to house the growing population of students. In early 2018, when the board voted to close the building, Mary Crapo housed the early childhood development center and alternative education classes. The building went up for sale, and there were talks of redevelopment, but after the main plan fell through, new discussions happened in December 2021. Demolition was proposed, and though many are against losing the historic building, there might not be another option if funds are not available.

The Mary Crapo is filled with history—and ghosts.

On the site GhostsofAmerica.com, a couple of former custodians chimed in about the strange and spooky happenings that occur at the Mary Crapo when the building is quiet and empty.

In 2019, former Mary Crapo student Janell Jagger and paranormal investigator Joe Yambrick were part of a team that did a ghost hunt in the old school. At the beginning of the investigation, two team members experienced intense emotional reactions in one of the rooms upstairs. "The emotional experience I had, that was a first for me," Yambrick said. "I felt a lot of anxiety and a lot of sadness, all within a split second. I never felt that before in my life." It was an eventful hunt. In the first room, the team explored, the batteries in the film crew's camera died, despite having had a full ten-hour charge. The basement was full of unexplained shadows crouching, creeping and moving along the old walls, shadows that seemed to gravitate toward the film crew. Yambrick said: "I definitely did not expect to find what we found. It was quite exciting, actually; and quite creepy. The experience as a whole was phenomenal."

8
CRANBERRIES CAFÉ (GOODRICH)

The Goodrich building that houses Cranberries Café started life as a general store in 1836. The building was rebuilt in 1917 using bricks from the Atlas brickmaking plant. Over the years, the building has housed the Goodrich Bank, an ice cream parlor, a tanning salon, a video rental shop, a trophy store and an antique store.

Patty Plant opened Cranberries in 1994 as a deli. A fire in 1998 caused extensive smoke damage to Cranberries, causing the café to be closed for a year and a half for renovations. During the renovations, they uncovered the original tin ceiling—along with something ghostly from the past.

Mitch Plant was working late one night on the ceiling restoration and got an odd feeling that he was no longer alone. He looked down from the ladder to spot a man standing there, nodding his head like he approved. Then, poof, the guy was just gone.

After that, there were other odd encounters: shadows darting between rooms, voices no one can account for and a spot in the basement that leaves people with an uneasy feeling.

In 2009, a group of paranormal investigators spent a couple of hours at Cranberries and recorded EVPs (electronic voice phenomenon) and readings on their devices that point to otherworldly activity. Davison filmmaker Jeffrey Jones filmed portions of his documentary *The Haunting Truth* at Cranberries. In his film, he examines area myths, legends and haunted places.

9
HAUNTED HOSPITALS

Hospitals, asylums and other medical institutions are places filled with immense emotion, including grief, horror, confusion and pain. Early medical treatments, specifically for those with mental issues, now seem like something out of a horror novel.

According to paranormal investigator Zak Bagans, principal host of the Travel Channel's *Ghost Adventures*, this kind of traumatic energy can create both residual and intelligent hauntings. Bagans explains that when an event (or multiple events) "imprints itself on the atmosphere" like a recording on a loop of film, the location plays back the traumatic events.

Intelligent hauntings are when the spirits present are intelligent and can interact with their surroundings. This type of haunting is created when a person is unable to "pass on" because of an emotional connection to the site, emotional ties to a person, intense trauma or unfinished business. In some cases, a spirit might not even realize they have died. This can occur when a death is sudden or unexpected, like an accident, murder or a medical emergency.

This explains why many old asylum and hospital locations are rife with reports of the paranormal.

A hospital is a liminal space—a threshold of transformation, a doorway between life and death. Liminal spaces are often considered to be haunted because they are locations that are neither here nor there; they are in-between pockets of life where we are stuck waiting or where we move between spaces.

Hurley Hospital postcard. *Author collection.*

There is also a theory that locations that experience a prolonged time frame of deaths (like hospitals, nursing homes and asylums) can open a revolving door to the other side through which spirits and other things can slip through. This can explain why so many locations have stories of residuals, intelligent hauntings and other sightings like shadow people and menacing entities.

Hurley Hospital (Flint)

James J. Hurley was born in London, England, on August 31, 1849. When he was twenty-two he arrived in New York before traveling to Grand Blanc, Michigan. He then made his way to Flint with just $1 in his pocket. Over the years, he became a wealthy man but never forgot growing up in poverty. Before his death, in April 1905, James J. Hurley donated $55,000 and land to the City of Flint to create a hospital for the poor. On December 19, 1908, Hurley Hospital opened with 40 beds, 6 bassinets and a staff of 8 nurses. A second story was built over the west wing in 1911. Through the years 1912 to 1919, the Hurley campus continued to grow with a nurses' home, an isolation unit, a maternity hospital and an expansion to 125 beds. In 1928, the original Hurley building was replaced with two 11-story towers, housing 432 beds with the most modern medical equipment available, for $2 million. This was just the first of Hurley's groundbreaking upgrades. After decades of world-class medical additions, new buildings and expanded services, the Hurley campus now sprawls across the city of Flint. In 2021, Hurley was named by *Newsweek* magazine as one of the World's Best Smart Hospitals. It ranked no. 1 in Michigan, no. 40 in the United States and no. 111 in the world.

Old blends with new, and tunnels run under many of the structures, connecting them so equipment and employees can easily move between buildings without going outside. The tunnels are one of the main locations where hauntings occur. Numerous employees are terrified to go into the tunnels; they swear the ghosts of former patients wander them, roaming forever under the hospital where they passed away. Former employees also claim a spirit haunts the psychiatric ward; this ghost likes to cause all kinds of havoc.

Tanya T., a paramedic in Flint, recounted a terrifying tale of a ghost in a mirror:

> *We have to walk down to the pharmacy at Hurley to get new drug boxes when we use certain medications. The pharmacy is located right where*

Hurley Hospital postcard. *Author collection.*

the newer part and the old hospital are joined. I always look in the bubble mirrors on the ceiling before rounding a corner to make sure that I do not bump into anyone. As I came to a corner, I looked up in the mirror and noticed a lady in dark clothing standing at the hall that goes into the old part of the hospital. I turned the corner, and she was not there. I stopped and did a double-take. I walked back around the corner looked in the mirror again. She was in the mirror. I peeked around the corner, and there was NO ONE THERE! But she was still in the mirror! I had chills. This happened again a few days later.

Another paramedic had weird occurrences with her ambulance while parked at Hurley. She mentioned that the rig once started on its own even though it was empty. And things in the back would fall off shelves and move around, but only while parked there. Out of all the locations she visits with the ambulance, Hurley is by far the spookiest.

McLaren Hospital (Flint)

McLaren Hospital began life in 1914 as a private 10-bed hospital on Harrison Street in Flint. The hospital was established by Lucy M. Elliot, MD, and Lillian Girard, RN. In 1919, it was reorganized and incorporated into a community nonprofit. A six-acre site on Lapeer Street was acquired and the residence renovated into a 29-bed Women's Hospital. A wing was added in 1929, increasing the capacity to 40 beds. A community fundraising event brought in millions of dollars in 1943 to build a new facility but because of the war and lack of materials, building was delayed. Construction at the current location on Ballenger Highway began in July 1949, and the new hospital opened its doors in October 1951 with a 243-bed capacity. It was named McLaren General Hospital after Margaret E. McLaren, RN, who served as the superintendent of the Women's Hospital for twenty-eight years. Over the years, new wings and buildings have been added, and a restructuring of the corporation changed the corporate name to McLaren Health Care, with the Flint hospital becoming McLaren Flint.

Many who have been inside McLaren mention the bad vibes or just the feeling that something is "off"; those can be chalked up to sadness, worry and grief that tie into why they are there. What about the strange shadows? Numerous patients at McLaren have mentioned shadows that dance across walls and dart into corners, even though they are alone in the room and there seems to be no plausible explanation for the shadows.

Hospitals are unnerving. The energy is chaotic. Fear, sadness, joy, grief—they all blend into purely chaotic energy. Roxanne had her daughter at McLaren in May 1999; due to complications, they had to stay for a couple of nights. Sleep was evasive; there were sounds, voices and shadows throughout the night that had no business being there. The second night Roxanne's mother-in-law stayed with her so she didn't have to be alone.

Wayne L. had surgery at McLaren in December 2020. As soon as he entered the hospital, he felt an unnatural chill. He arrived in the pre-op room and, noticing a shadow out of the corner of his eye, turned to look, but nothing was there. An overwhelming feeling that he was being watched washed over him. He spotted another shadow dart across the wall. He was in a room alone; there was no source for this shadow. Finally, the nurse arrived to wheel him to the operating room. On the way there, in what seemed like a never-ending hallway, he heard whispers, like multiple people having quiet conversations, but when he looked around it was just him and the nurse, alone in the hall. In the operating room, before going under anesthesia he once again spotted a shadow out of the corner of his eye.

In December 2016, Kristeen W. was placed in a room in the older part of the building after surgery. She fell asleep as soon as she arrived in her room, only to wake up to a voice that said, "Well, hello there." But the room was empty. Several times, her television turned on by itself. When a nurse came in to check on her, Kristeen joked that there was a ghost in the room. The nurse laughed and replied, "Oh, I could tell you some stories." After that, Kristeen made her husband stay with her until she was released.

WALTER WINCHESTER HOSPITAL (FLINT)

The location started life as the Genesee County Infirmary in 1927, a place where the county's poor could receive medical services. In 1941, the medical director of the Genesee County Welfare Department, Dr. Walter H. Winchester, became the medical superintendent of the infirmary. He held that position until his retirement in 1962. Before his retirement, the hospital was renamed the Walter Winchester Hospital in his honor in 1961.

By 1969, funding cuts forced the Winchester to merge with Genesee Memorial Hospital. But the merge couldn't keep them up and running, so their doors closed in 1970. In 1972, the building was converted to offices for the Genesee County Department of Social Services. The county moved out in 1983. After that, the building sat empty and unused for years. At one point, rumors indicated the site was to be transformed into a VA hospital, but that never happened.

Businessman and future Flint mayor Don Williamson purchased the property in 1990. He never did anything with it, and urban decay took over.

By the mid-1990s, the location had become a popular hangout for teenagers, vandals and vagrants. Located right next to Sunset Hills Cemetery, which features the haunting legend of the Crack the Whip statue, the two locations went hand in hand when it came to ghost stories and urban legends. Teenagers in the 1990s dared one another to sneak into the cemetery at night and try on the shoe of the Crack the Whip statue. Kids also loved to wander around the ruins of the Walter Winchester Hospital. Teens would party there all the time. Rumors swirled that devil worship and occult sacrifices took place at the site. By the late 1990s, the hospital was no more than a hulking shell covered in graffiti and littered with trash.

But it wasn't the trash or the graffiti that was the problem. It was the gut-wrenching, hair-standing-on-end feeling of horror that sent many running from the site. No one knows what resided in those horrid ruins, but if you were smart, you steered clear of them.

In 1998, Williamson sold the land to New Calvary Cemetery, and thankfully, that creepy shell of a building was torn down soon after. All that remains now is empty land. New Calvary Cemetery plans to eventually build an annex at the location.

The Old Hospital on Pine Street (Lapeer)

Peter Van Dyke built his three-story French Second Empire mansion on Pine Street in 1875. It started as a gorgeous private home with high ceilings; large rooms; cherry, walnut and oak woodwork; and a walnut spiral staircase leading to the second level.

Van Dyke sold the house to Samuel Tomlinson, editor of the *Lapeer Clarion*. John Williams was the third owner, followed by Robert White, then owner of Lapeer Brick and Tile. Records indicate the sisters Frances and Mary Ellen Hunter bought the Pine Street building in 1923 from Clarence Butler. Frances Hunter was a hospital supervisor in Marlette at the time. It opened

Old Hospital on Pine. *Photo by Roxanne Rhoads.*

as a nine-bed hospital on September 6, 1924. Later, the capacity doubled to eighteen beds. It was used as a medical facility for twenty-nine years until August 1, 1953, when the new Lapeer Hospital was being built. It has been an apartment building since the 1960s.

There are quite a few rumors about the location being haunted—as often happens with beautiful old houses and even more so with places that were once hospitals.

Former Lapeer resident Justin Arnold said the building has intense energy:

> *About ten years ago I went with some friends to check it out. Upon walking up to the house I could feel its energy, almost standing in protest. I clearly saw the old hospital painted a dark red all over with white accents. The next day I drove by and was shocked to see the colors were opposite to what I had seen the night before. The building was now all white with red accents, which hinted to me that this property may exist on many different planes.*

In a 2011 article that appeared in the *County Press*, a woman named Kimberly, who once lived in the building, was convinced the place was haunted. She constantly heard scratching noises in the walls and the sound of a little girl giggling and calling her name.

"I was waking up in bed in the main room. I was in that lucid, almost wide awake but not-quite-there yet state," she said.

> *The little girl, Elizabeth, was standing at the side of my bed, staring me right in the eyes. She was wearing a light blue dress and had very dark hair. She looked to be between five and seven years old. Then the nurse came up to the end of the hallway from the bathroom—about five or so feet—and told her to come back, called her by name. The nurse's name was Virginia. I think she had a name tag on.* [She was] *wearing traditional old-fashioned nurse garb. She took the little girl and they went back toward the bathroom, away from the main area. I couldn't breathe the whole time this was happening.*

The night Kimberly moved out of the apartment she saw a full apparition on the stairs between the first and second floors.

Another woman, Naomi, also had strange experiences living in the apartments at Pine Street. Turns out she lived in the same apartment that Kimberly once inhabited. Naomi also felt strange sensations and heard weird noises, including the voice of a little girl.

It seems that former patients and hospital staff still wander the halls of this beautiful old building.

10

CREEPY CEMETERIES

Cities of the dead often have numerous tales of hauntings attached to them, but how many are simply stories fueled by overactive imaginations? Why would a ghost want to haunt their final resting place instead of a place they loved in life or even the location where they died? Troy Taylor, author of *Beyond the Grave: The History of America's Most Haunted Graveyards*, believes that cemetery hauntings happen due to events that occur after death, not before or at the time of. "Cemeteries gain a reputation for being haunted for reasons that include the desecration of the dead and grave robbery, unmarked or forgotten burials, natural disasters that disturb resting places, or sometimes even because the deceased was not properly buried."

Most of the cemeteries and graveyards in Genesee and Lapeer Counties are quite peaceful with nary a ghost story to be found. Some of the more active cemeteries in the area—Avondale, Glenwood and Sunset Hills—were featured in *Haunted Flint*. Each of those can fall into one of the aforementioned categories. Avondale has quite a few unmarked graves along with gravestones that may or may not have bodies under them; it has also experienced quite a bit of vandalism. Glenwood has unmarked graves and graves that have become nameless. Glenwood and Avondale are both old, with graves dating back to the first settlers in the area. Sunset Hills is known for the statue Crack the Whip, which garners unwanted attention and nighttime trespassers; this may cause unrest among the dead buried there.

CRONK CEMETERY (FLINT TOWNSHIP)

The Cronk Cemetery is a quaint little cemetery that looks picturesque in the fall. It was originally established in the 1800s as a family plot. It was formerly known as the West Flint Cemetery. Cronk is now maintained by the Charter Township of Flint. It is located on Beecher Road between Elms and Linden Roads.

Cronk is a peaceful cemetery full of trees and shade. One sunny autumn day, Roxanne decided to visit the cemetery. During the cemetery visit, she felt a strange tug on her sleeve while she was taking photos. It was the type of tug you feel when a small child walks up to you and tries to get your attention. She walked in the direction of the tug but never felt anything out of the ordinary or saw what she might have been directed to. Nothing showed up in any of the photos from that area. She never figured out what the ghostly tug meant or what it wanted her to see.

She did find an odd little snowman on what looked to be a child's grave. She felt it was best to leave it undisturbed.

Cronk Cemetery. *Photo by Roxanne Rhoads.*

NEW CALVARY CATHOLIC CEMETERY (FLINT)

New Calvary Catholic Cemetery established in 1928 is in the same area as Sunset Hills and River Rest. In fact, they all join together and it's hard to see where one ends and the other begins unless you pay close attention to the change in grave markers and statuary.

New Calvary is larger than Old Calvary, which was established in 1847 but dwarfed by Sunset Hills. New Calvary is where most Catholics in the Flint area are interred, including Pulitzer Prize–winning journalist William Gallagher. The cemetery consists of a grassy slope dotted with small trees ending at a large mausoleum that backs up to the grounds of Sunset Hills.

Paranormal investigator Maria Holt-Aistrop says New Calvary is full of paranormal energy and spirits that want to communicate. Make sure your recorder is turned on before you get out of your vehicle. And be careful, the ghosts may try to go home with you. Maria encountered spirits that tried to get into her vehicle.

PINE RUN CEMETERY (VIENNA TOWNSHIP)

Pine Run is a small unincorporated community within Vienna Township; many often think it is part of Clio. The cemetery was established sometime after 1833 when the area was first settled. Pine Run is said to be haunted by a family of spirits—a man, woman and child who are buried there. People have reported seeing them walking around the cemetery together. Others have felt a strange presence in the cemetery and get the feeling they are being watched. Several investigators have experienced the sudden failure of electrical devices such as flashlights and ghost hunting tools. Even vehicles have experienced mechanical failures such as a suddenly dead battery or a car that simply refused to move even though it was in gear.

EVERGREEN CEMETERY (GRAND BLANC)

Evergreen Cemetery is also known as Whigville Cemetery. It is well kept and looks rather modern and ordinary, but some graves date to the late 1800s and there is a public vault that dates to 1888.

There are rumors that people have seen bizarre shadows, orbs and strange lights in this Hill Road cemetery.

One evening, the superintendent spotted strange flickering lights and went to investigate. He encountered a group of robed figures holding candles and chanting. Upon seeing him, they disappeared into the darkness of the night. Many staff members have seen weird shadows floating through the cemetery and have heard phantom footsteps. One woman who worked in the main office would regularly hear the bells tinkle as if someone walked into the office, but when she looked around no one was there and the door was closed.

Paranormal investigators have had numerous orbs and mists appear in their photos, though nothing substantial has been seen.

DAVISON CEMETERY (DAVISON)

The Davison Cemetery is a mix of old and new plots. Quite a few dating to the mid- to late 1800s blend right in with modern burials. The cemetery has a reputation for ghostly activity. Even the cemetery's Google reviews mention ghosts. One reviewer said, "The ghosts are what's up and very chill. Probably an excellent place to have a séance." Another reviewer said, "Spooky vibes. Friendly ghosts."

Paranormal investigator Maria Holt-Aistrop had an interesting encounter there: "We heard growling like a wild animal, but not. There was a ball of light that followed us as well."

Roxanne and her daughter visited the Potter Road cemetery on a sunny autumn day. Headstones with familiar local names like Goodrich, Bentley and Sloan reside in the Davison Cemetery, and the feeling of historical significance hung in the air. But there was no paranormal activity, just intrusive noise from a nearby construction site.

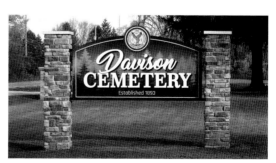

Davison Cemetery. *Photo by Roxanne Rhoads.*

MOUNT HOPE CEMETERY (LAPEER)

Established in 1847, the Mount Hope Cemetery sits on twenty-five picturesque acres with roughly twenty-six thousand grave spaces, many of which feature familiar names from Lapeer's history—White, Hart, Turrill, John Treadway Rich (who served as governor of Michigan from 1893 to 1897) and Judge William Brown Williams (1849–1923), who played an important role in the 1918 Michigan Supreme Court case *Haynes v. Lapeer Circuit Judge*, which protects the institutionalized from sterilization.

Locals consider it to be a hotbed of paranormal activity. Many have reported ghostly sightings, strange voices and odd lights coming from this cemetery. Justin Arnold recounted a story he heard:

> *Years and years ago kids were playing in the cemetery and were approached by an elderly man in a tan Buick. He offered them some gum and stated he was the caretaker. Later the boys told their mother what had happened, and it turned out the caretaker had passed years earlier. She knew this because he drove a tan Buick. The eeriest thing was the boys still had the wrappers from the gum in their pockets.*

A local photographer took senior portraits of twins between the large oaks in the center of the cemetery. When the photos were processed, white and green orbs surrounded the twins. The twins had relatives buried in the cemetery—perhaps they wanted to take part in the photo shoot.

Mt. Hope Cemetery Gates. *Photo by Roxanne Rhoads.*

Many residents neighboring the cemetery have reported ghostly apparitions and strange encounters. One woman who lived on Liberty Street would often see a "tall shadow man whose neck is either twisted or broken."

There's an old legend that skeletons are gatekeepers of the cemetery. To experience them, you must go after dark. Start on M-24 and turn on Park Street driving toward the cemetery. Move slowly toward the cemetery gates and look directly through the main gate. As you drive very slowly toward the gates, keep looking straight ahead; the stone towers and metal will reflect your lights, and in your peripheral vision, you can see the columns turn into skeletons.

South Dryden Pioneer Cemetery (Lapeer County)

The South Dryden Pioneer Cemetery is also known as Foot Cemetery and Miller Cemetery. It is southwest of Dryden about a half hour east of Flint. Established in the mid-1800s, this cemetery is home to some of the Dryden area's earliest settlers.

At the intersection of Rochester and Casey Roads near where the cemetery is located, there is a story that three teens out joyriding were involved in a fatal accident one night. Now their spirits haunt the cemetery and the intersection. The area is plagued by ghostly headlights that come toward you and then suddenly disappear, the gut-wrenching sounds of squealing tires and crunching metal with no source and disembodied voices crying for help.

Locals often mention seeing glowing orbs and strange lights moving among the headstones like someone is walking through the cemetery with an old lantern. Others have seen a dark shadowy figure that seems to be a guardian lurking in the back of the cemetery. Several visitors claimed they were chased away by the dark shadow figure.

11

THE LINDEN HOTEL

The Linden Hotel is the oldest continuously working business in Genesee County.

The first white settlers in the Linden area arrived around 1835. Seth Sadler and Consider Warner both arrived around 1836, and Eben Harris followed in 1838. In 1840, Warner and Harris platted the land. The new settlement was first named Warner Mills. The hotel was built at the corner of East Broad and Bridge Streets. In the beginning, it was called the Exchange and was well known for its hospitality, which featured delicious meals and fine lodging. When the railroad came through, the hotel became even more popular. Linden was incorporated as a village in 1871.

By the time the age of the automobile rolled around in the early twentieth century, lodging in small towns wasn't necessary anymore. Owner Ed Dumanois created a fine-dining destination. Small groups would motor in from Flint and other areas for dinner parties at the Exchange.

In 1921, Dumanois sold the Exchange to James and Emma Reip, who changed the name to House of Plenty. They catered to the elite, and their guest book featured well-known names in Michigan Society. Private dining rooms were filled with governors, senators and automobile company presidents.

In 1954, after over 120 years on the corner, the hotel was moved to its current location on Broad Street.

Jack Furry purchased the hotel in 1993. It continued offering lodging until 1998. Around 2016, the upper rooms were remodeled and turned into the Crow's Nest, a sports bar for the twenty-one and over crowd. Sadly, in January 2021, Jack Furry passed away, but his two daughters continue to operate the Linden Hotel.

The hauntings seem to have started in 1998. Linden was holding Civil War Days, and soldiers dressed in their Union uniforms were on the second floor of the hotel when a photo was taken. In the photo, a Confederate soldier appears—faceless, holding a sword or staff. Everyone swears there were no soldiers dressed in Confederate uniforms there. No one can identify the man.

Since then, other strange things have happened: keys jingle without being touched, salt shakers crash to the floor, employees feel tugs on their shirts by unseen hands, shadows move in empty rooms and a TV likes to turn on by itself. Numerous paranormal groups have done investigations. Brenda Mikulka of South East Michigan Ghost Hunters Society captured an incredible photo of a ghostly young woman with blond hair dressed in a white nightgown standing on her tiptoes.

The DJ booth in the sports bar on the second floor is an intense area that sensitives can't stomach. Just one foot in can leave you feeling ill and out of whack. Former owner Jack Furry said he knew who was haunting the space and that he'd been there for a while. The spirit is thought to be a man named Charles (Chuck) who had a room at the hotel for an extended period of time. He liked the place so much he decided to come back after death. It's not known if he died at the hotel. A psychic from the South East Michigan Ghost Hunters Society made contact with him; Chuck said he enjoyed the hotel and wanted to remain instead of crossing over. Contact was also made with a young woman who said she had been having an affair with one of the hotel's regular guests in the 1800s. A fire broke out in her room, and she died from smoke inhalation.

David Tucker of Greater Michigan Paranormal Investigations left the hotel with an interesting video. Many other investigators have found "proof" of hauntings. It seems that several spirits lurk in the hotel in addition to Chuck and the ghostly young woman.

12

FENTON

In 1834, Clark Dibble made his way through the wilderness from Shiawassee to Grumlaw (Grand Blanc). By mistake, he found himself on the White Lake Trail. From there, he went north and came upon a spot on the Shiawassee River where several Indian trails came together. He fell in love with the beauty of the location and decided to build there. He encouraged others to join him. In 1836, Clark Dibble sold his entire town of Dibbleville to Robert LeRoy and William M. Fenton, which they platted and renamed Fentonville.

The city's name change to Fentonville is rumored to have occurred thanks to a high-spirited card game played by candlelight and fueled by whiskey. This legendary game has been immortalized in a bronze sculpture called *The Game* created by artist Oleg Kedria and unveiled on the grounds of the Fenton Community and Cultural Center on October 5, 2017. Fenton folklore states that on August 24, 1837, a card game decided the name of the city. William M. Fenton, Robert LeRoy and Benjamin Rockwell played for naming rights. After Fenton's winning hand for the city, they went on to play for the naming rights to the streets.

Robert LeRoy built a hotel in 1837 and later became postmaster. William Fenton went on to become lieutenant governor of Michigan. In 1850, Fentonville became the northernmost point on the Detroit, Grand Haven and Milwaukee Railroad. This made Fentonville a bustling location for commerce and transportation. The iconic Fenton Hotel was built in 1856. From 1837 to 1886, the post office used the name Fentonville, even though

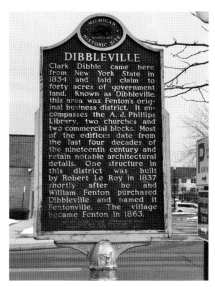 

Left: Dibbleville Historical Marker. *Photo by Ilona Curry*.

Right: The Game Placard. *Photo by Roxanne Rhoads*.

The Game Statue. *Photo by Roxanne Rhoads*.

in 1863, the settlement was incorporated as the Village of Fenton. It was promoted to the City of Fenton in 1964.

Today, many of Fenton's original homes and buildings still stand, and more than a handful are rumored to be haunted. An old home on High Street is plagued by the sounds of classical music in the middle of the night. Numerous investigations have found no source for the sounds. However, research into the house found that two ladies who lived in the home almost one hundred years ago taught piano. A home on South Adelaide Street had misty faces that would appear in a mirror. Another home on Adelaide suffered from the sounds of odd footsteps, hands trying to push them down stairs and a heavy front door that would fly open for no reason. A Main Street home had a candle that would not stay in the candelabra. Residents would see the candle flip out of the center holder and fly across the room. Visitors to another home on Main Street would often hear the ghostly cries of a child. A woman who lived in a house on Shiawassee awoke one August night to an apparition of a woman with flowing hair wearing a long gown. A year later, she awoke to the ghostly sight of a misty man bathed in moonlight.

Several businesses in downtown Fenton boast a ghost or two. The old grain elevator, turned into Red Fox Outfitters, which closed in 2020, has

Grain Elevator. *Photo by Roxanne Rhoads.*

been rumored to be filled with eerie occupants who like to slam doors and create chaos. Fenton's Open Book has a ghost that likes to spin the rotating displays and knock books off shelves. The bookstore resides in the historic building known as the Andrews Block at the corner of South LeRoy Street and West Shiawassee Avenue. It was built by C. Andrews in 1867 and added to the State Register of Historic Sites in January 1976.

Norman's House

A historic home on East Shiawassee in downtown Fenton has quite the reputation for being Fenton's most haunted home. Built in the late 1800s, Norman Hough and his wife, Elizabeth, resided there for at least thirty-two years, until Norman passed away in the home on April 27, 1926, at the age of ninety-three. Norman was a deacon at Fenton's Baptist Church for fifty-two years. Unexplained occurrences are a rather common thing in this house.

An article published by the *Flint Journal* in 1979 focused on the Brumbacks' and the Yacks' ghostly encounters. The Brumacks were the owners of the home at the time the article was written. It started with Marilyn Brumback cleaning windows one day when she heard footsteps upstairs. She knew she was alone in the house, but her dog ran to the bottom of the stairs and started barking. She was so scared she ran outside, not sure of what to do. Finally, she got the courage and went back inside, where she found no one. That was her first encounter with the ghost.

Throughout the Brumbacks' time in the house, they experienced quite a few "Norman" encounters: creaky footsteps from an empty floor, doors opening by themselves and plenty of strange bumps and bangs. They got together with former residents, the Yacks, and talked about "Norman." Betty Yack gave the ghost the name Norman after discovering Reverend Norman Hough passed away in the house from a stroke in 1926.

The Yacks dealt with pictures that refused to stay on the walls, and they often heard loud crashes like the sounds of windows shattering. They would search the house from top to bottom and never found a source for the sounds.

Marilyn Brumback tried to hang a picture in the kitchen; every time she would hang it up, it would fall. Finally, she thought it was secure and turned to leave the kitchen; it didn't just fall, it flew off the wall, sailed across the room and knocked an ashtray to the floor. She decided Norman did not like her décor choices. She did not try to hang the picture up again. She had already dealt with a mirror that fell and shattered for no apparent reason. James Brumback, Marilyn's husband, pulled up floorboards to try to find a source for the creaks but came up empty. Betty Yack's husband, Allan, would often hear the distant sounds of classical music when he was working in the basement. He would search and search for the music but could never pinpoint where it was coming from.

Other members of the Brumback family experienced strange noises and odd occurrences. One night while sitting with friends, a bone-jarring crash shook them. It sounded like a car had slammed right into their home. They jumped up and dashed outside to find…nothing.

The house was quite popular on Halloween. High school students would approach the Brumback teen exclaiming, "Oh my god, you live in the haunted house!"

The Brumbacks eventually got used to sharing their space with Norman. When something strange would happen, like a locked door swinging open or the toilet paper being unrolled across the bathroom, they would just say, "Norman, knock it off."

Over the years, many people have lived in the house. Some reported they never had anything odd happen. Others dealt with many strange happenings: electronics that would turn off and on by themselves, music with no source, voices in the night, things falling off walls—including a mirror that would continually fall off the wall but never break—a door that opened by itself and a rocking chair that liked to rock when no one was sitting in it. Several people have even spotted the apparition of Norman himself wandering about the old place, most often on the front porch.

The home was remodeled and sold to new owners in December 2021.

Fenton Seminary

Before its demolition in 2015, the Fenton Seminary, which stood at the corner of 309 High Street and State Road, was one of Fenton's most haunted locations and definitely the one with the spookiest aesthetic.

Roxanne first discovered this haunting beauty back in 1990. Her boyfriend at the time grew up in the Fenton area and wanted to show her the spooky place that all the kids were afraid of. He told her about the rumors the kids used to share about how haunted the place was. It seems the house was bought and sold numerous times, but no one would stay in it very long.

Fenton Seminary/Baptist Home. *Author collection.*

Roxanne and her boyfriend drove there one night. The visage of this hulking stone structure against the backdrop of darkness was utterly terrifying. She was so scared that she wouldn't even let him pull into the driveway. Roxanne doesn't spook easily, and it is rare for her to have such intense feelings of fear, but when she does, she knows to trust her gut. Even back then, she knew that something was wrong and she shouldn't even step foot on the property.

Even though the place terrified her, she was fascinated by its history. She told her friend Jenny about the building, and Jenny had her cousin, who was in college studying architecture and design, contact the real estate agent. He was given the keys to the place so he could sketch it. She invited Roxanne to join them in the exploration.

Roxanne returned during daylight hours to visit the spooky stone structure. They walked around the main levels and explored a bit. It was remarkably clean for a place that had been empty for years. She planned to explore the entire building, but after a rocking chair started rocking by itself in one of the second-floor bedrooms and a door slammed on her in another room, she decided to cut the exploration short. That was enough spooky for her. She didn't get to see the basement or the sub-basement, which Jenny said had a stream running through it. Later, Roxanne saw some of the photos Jenny took. There were so many orbs, weird lights and strange blurry smudges in them that none of them came out clear.

Several years later, another friend told Roxanne about his experiences in a haunted house in Fenton. Turns out it was the old seminary. He detailed a story about a group of teens that would sneak in and party in the place. They had a nice spot on one of the upper floors. One night, he needed a place to crash and ended up in the old place all alone. He heard a strange and creaky squealing noise, and then a small door on the wall popped open. It was a dumbwaiter, and something jumped out at him. He didn't get a good look at it; he just took off running and flew down the stairs. Whatever it was had sharp claws that tore the back of his T-shirt to tatters. He showed Roxanne the shirt that he had kept as a reminder to never return to that cursed place. The shirt looked like Freddy Krueger had raked his razor-sharp glove across it.

Locations that used to be seminaries, asylums, hospitals and nursing homes usually report tons of supernatural activity, probably from all the people who lived and died in the location. Even if nothing "bad" happened there, residual energy builds up. Roxanne's theory is that doorways are created in locations where many people go in and out of this world. Like a hospital, where people are born and die every day, a gateway opens, and sometimes something might slip through that shouldn't.

The ten-thousand-square-foot building was originally built to be a Baptist school in 1868. It stood on twenty-five acres of land. Around 1886, it opened

Fenton Seminary. *Photo by Andrew Jameson CC.*

as a retirement home for Baptist ministers, their wives, widows and orphans from the states of Michigan, Ohio, Indiana, Illinois and Wisconsin. It was used as such until about 1938.

In 1899, a kitchen fire gutted the interior and destroyed the roof and the original two-story veranda with its balustrades and divided front steps, causing around $25,000 to $35,000 in damages. Reverend Snyder was fatally burned, and a Mr. Engles, aged eighty-one, was badly injured after jumping out of an upper-story window. The *Flint Daily News* reported on February 21, 1899, that the fire "originated from the explosion of a gasoline stove on the third floor, and spread with such rapidity that by the time the fire department reached the scene the upper part of the building was all in flames."

The three-story stone structure with thirty-two-inch stone walls was originally constructed in the Second Empire style with a mansard roof, dormers, rounded arch windows and a double stairway front porch. During the building's reconstruction in 1900, the porch was altered; the front stairway changed to a single flight, and the third story was eliminated and replaced by a truncated hip roof. The new roof featured a centrally placed gable dormer, which was flanked by metal dormers.

For a short time in the 1940s, the building was a learning center for kids. It was later used as an apartment building. In the 1950s, the elderly filled the halls while it was a nursing home. Several times, it was privately owned, but residents never lasted long. It sat mostly vacant from 1967 to the mid-1990s.

In November 1982, it was added to the National Register of Historic Places. For years, it was one of Fenton's most prominent nineteenth-century structures.

Penny Crane purchased the building in the mid-1990s with hopes of returning it to its original glory. First, she restored the wood house adjacent to the seminary as a place for her to live. There was an underground passageway from the house to the seminary. Crane mentioned in an interview that there were several underground tunnels and passageways on the property. Soon after purchasing it in 1995, she opened the monstrous structure to the public as a haunted house. With every window and doorway closed off from the outside world, the interior was dark and shrouded in mystery. It must have been terrifying. The multistory monster would have been so easy to get lost in.

In an article from May 2013 in the *Tri-City Times*, Crane said: "I didn't believe in any ghosts or spirits but I sure do now."

Fenton city officials quickly closed the haunt's doors and condemned it until the proper permits could be approved for renovation. Crane fought with the city for years to lift the condemned status so she could transform the

Left: Baptist Memorial. *Photo by Roxanne Rhoads.*

Right: All that remains of the seminary. *Photo by Roxanne Rhoads.*

monastery into a usable facility. For over twenty years, she struggled to try to renovate the building. She even tried to walk away from it once, but the ownership reverted right back to her.

The hulking building would have been the perfect setting for a horror movie. People would get spooked just looking at it. Dark, decrepit and filled with creepy corners and spooky shadows, it was an entity all its own. At one point, the massive stone stairs led to a chained-off entrance while a tattered "Condemned" sign hung from a ground-level door and a "No Trespassing" sign hung on one of the windows.

In 2004, the building had a fire.

In November 2013, the building was severely damaged by storms, and a portion of it crumbled. In 2014, it was further damaged by storms. Also in 2014, the county took ownership due to $20,000 of back taxes that were owed. In January 2015, the City of Fenton took ownership, it was deemed dangerous by a structural engineer and was demolished in September 2015.

Bricks and other materials from the old seminary have been used to erect a monument that now stands in Section B of the Oakwood Cemetery in Fenton.

The corner where the building once stood is now just an empty lot, but the menace remains. Are the underground tunnels still there hiding under the dirt and grass, or were they filled in when the buildings were torn down?

A sense of unease hung in the air when Roxanne visited the lot to take photos one sunny afternoon. Her first attempt didn't work because her phone seized up, making a weird noise, and the camera closed. She had to get her actual camera out of the bag to snap a few shots. A few days later, her phone died for good. Coincidence? Maybe. Maybe not.

THE FENTON HOTEL TAVERN AND GRILLE

The Fenton Hotel Tavern and Grille is the most haunted bar in Michigan according to Thrillest.com. In 2019, Thrillest rounded up seventeen of the most haunted bars and restaurants in the United States, and the Fenton Hotel made the list.

The hotel was built in 1856 soon after the railroad made its way to Fentonville in 1855. Gazetteer, Seed and Flint were the builders and owners of what they named the Vermont House. In 1868, Abner Roberts became proprietor of the newly named Fenton House. It became the DeNio in 1882, when D.W. DeNio purchased the hotel and gave it a facelift, complete with new wallpaper and furnishings. The Carpediem Club organized a fancy grand opening event with over two hundred guests. It was a roaring success. The DeNio House was one of the first Fentonville locations to get a telephone. DeNio continued to improve the accommodations. By 1886, it had a barn that could house one hundred horses and a hall thirty by eighty feet for public events. A Mr. Hurd became the new proprietor in 1898 and restored the Fenton House name.

In 1916, T.J. Dumanois, owner of the nearby Linden Hotel, purchased the hotel. Soon after his purchase, Prohibition shut it down. After the repeal of Prohibition in 1933, the hotel reopened under the management of Arthur and Margaret Dumanois, T.J.'s son and wife. It is said that the Fenton Hotel was the first business to receive a liquor license in Genesee County after Prohibition.

Over the years, the hotel continued to change hands, and the focus shifted to it being a restaurant and event center instead of a hotel. The location received a state historical marker in 1971. In 1997, Nick and Peggy Sorise bought the building and renamed it the Fenton Hotel opening it as a fine-dining establishment. In 2006, the Sorises celebrated the building's 150th anniversary with renovations and an updated name: the Fenton Hotel Tavern and Grille.

Today the brick building still stands at the corner of North Leroy and Main, looking much the same as it did in the nineteenth century. The only real difference is the front porch was torn off in 1904 by a team of runaway horses.

The hotel has managed to keep a tight grip on its past. The dining room still features its original tin ceilings, and the foyer probably looks similar to the way it appeared in the early days of the railroad. It's easy to envision ghostly guests appearing in their nineteenth-century finery.

The second floor features a tiled ballroom, restrooms and a room that once belonged to longtime custodian Emery. He worked there when the business was still renting rooms. The building stopped being a hotel in 1965.

But Emery never left—he still lingers long after his death. Strange things are usually attributed to him: tools being moved, lights being turned on and off, a vacuum that would constantly get unplugged, a popcorn maker that would turn on late at night, but the scariest thing is the footsteps many employees hear from upstairs after closing time. Heavy footsteps reverberating off the tin ceiling, and thumps on the walls are nighttime occurrences that get blamed on Emery.

Emery's not the only spirit roaming the place. There are numerous spirits, like the phantom hugger who has been seen embracing staff when they felt no one. One employee would often hear someone calling her name even though she was alone. Then there's the naughty entity who likes to break wine glasses and another who likes to grab the derrières of female waitstaff.

The bar and the dining room are both hot spots of activity. During December, ghostly activity increases; the Christmas decorations and events really seem to get everyone in the spirit of the season.

The third floor also has its fair share of spectral activity. Back in the day, the third floor featured the cheaper rooms of the hotel, which were often used by the town's working girls. Rumor has it one working girl hanged herself in the third stall of the restroom. Occasionally, women have reported strange feelings and cold spots in that stall; one woman even reported that she felt someone touch her hair.

The Fenton Hotel. *Photo by Roxanne Rhoads.*

Several full apparitions have been spotted, including a black cat, a bearded man outside a second-story window, a tall man in a top hat and the most popular ghost of the establishment, the man at table 32 who continues to crave Jack Daniels in his afterlife. Numerous times a man at table 32 has been seen by staff and patrons. He orders a Jack and Coke only to disappear into the ether before the waitstaff can return with his drink. Sometimes he is alone; other times he piggybacks off the drink orders of other people seated at the table, only for the waitstaff to return with drinks and discover there was no man at the table who ordered a Jack and Coke.

A reporter became personally haunted after investigating the Fenton Hotel for a Halloween article. Her husband shared the story with Roxanne under the terms that they both remain anonymous.

The story starts with a woman who had always been "gifted." She used this gift to become a successful tarot card reader; she could see, hear and feel "things." But for years, this gift had been rather quiet—until the couple visited the Fenton Hotel. They used a recorder during the investigation and caught the voice of someone mocking them. They returned to record more, and this time the voice said the woman's name. Next, they investigated the Holly Hotel, and they recorded the same voice calling her name. Whatever entity they encountered in Fenton was now following them. Strange things started happening in their home. They moved, and the hauntings continued. She would see shadow people and dark figures. They both saw doppelgangers of each other with slack mouths and black eyes. Voices would whisper in the night, and doors would open by themselves. The couple would wake up with strange scratches on their bodies. Finally, they called in a paranormal investigation team that captured upward of seventy EVPs. One voice kept saying it wanted to "take her light."

The Fenton Hotel's spirits have been referred to as guests who can check out but never leave, but something left and followed this woman home.

COLWELL OPERA HOUSE

The Horton-Colwell Opera House that is now in Crossroads Village once stood at the corner of Leroy and Caroline Streets in Fenton. The opera house was built in 1869 by Dexter Horton and David Colwell. It housed the Fenton General Store and post office on the first floor. The Fenton Opera House was on the second floor.

Colwell Opera House, first building on right. *Author collection.*

The Fenton Opera House was quite a hub of social activity for the village of Fenton. Susan B. Anthony visited in 1870. In 1883, the Fenton Ladies' Band rented the opera house on Tuesdays and Saturdays, offering a rink for the new fad of roller skating. It cost ten cents to skate and five cents for skate rental.

The annual Knights Templar's Ball was held there, along with graduations, school plays and outside entertainment, including a traveling production of *Uncle Tom's Cabin*, a visit by Tom Thumb and Mrs. Thumb in 1879, and a demonstration of Thomas Edison's Kinetoscope in 1887. Over the years, the opera house was used by churches, schools and fraternal organizations. In 1890, it was renovated with a new stage floor, and two dressing rooms were added.

In May 1910, Grace Colwell hosted a Halley's Comet party on the roof of the building.

One of the most interesting inhabitants of the building was the Independent Order of Odd Fellows. It was the first fraternal organization to let women in when it formed the Daughters of Rebekah in September 1851. In recent years, the Odd Fellows organization made the news when it was discovered that it had skeletons in the closets. Literally. Many of the order's old buildings have revealed hidden secrets during renovations. Numerous times, someone has pulled up a floorboard or opened a hidden

Odd Fellows Rebekah membership card for Roxanne's grandmother. *Author collection.*

space and come face to face with a skeleton or a coffin full of bones. So far, skeletons have turned up in New York, Virginia, California, Maryland, Oklahoma, Indiana, Minnesota, Pennsylvania, Texas and Nebraska. Like other fraternal organizations, the Odd Fellows use certain "secret" rites, rituals and codes. Members claim that their initiation ritual, which used a skeleton, was meant to instill a "visceral awareness of one's own mortality" in the initiate by having them stare death in the face. This was supposed to encourage the member to live a virtuous life. An anonymous account of the ceremony published in 1846 describes how an initiate must face a skeleton "kept rattling by means of wires," while current members tell him, "What thou art he was. What he is thou wilt surely be."

In the brickwork of the old Fenton building, you can still see "FLT," which is one of the symbols for the Odd Fellows; it stands for the order's motto, "Friendship, Love and Truth." There are no reports of skeletons, bones or coffins being found when the building was dismantled and moved to Crossroads Village. No reports of macabre findings were ever made by any previous owners of the building, either.

C.A. Damon owned the opera house in the early 1900s, followed by Mrs. W.P. Cook in the 1910s, who renamed it Cook's Opera House. Later, Frank Granger became the owner. He also owned the Fenton hardware store and was mayor of Fenton. His daughter, Mrs. Frank Vaclavik of Holland, Michigan, inherited the building after his death. In the 1930s, the opera house was once again used for roller skating until the floor was condemned. It was last used in 1975 as a dime store. The structure was torn down and rebuilt at Crossroads with some of the original bricks, ceiling beams and window casements. It debuted in the 1978 season and was completed in 1980. The A.J. Phillips Fenton Historical Museum in Fenton displays several artifacts from the original opera house.

Colwell Opera House at Christmas. *Photo by Roxanne Rhoads.*

The old opera house is the epitome of a liminal space. The building is stuck reliving its glory days with tourists at Crossroads Village, sometimes the past collides with the present. Out of the corner of your eye, you may catch a glimpse of a former patron in fancy late nineteenth-century attire.

Theaters are often thought to be haunted by actors, directors and staff. The Colwell Opera House is no exception. There's a story passed around among Crossroads Village employees that a female spirit lurks on the stairs going up to the second floor. Rumor has it she died when she tripped and fell down the stairs while the building was still in Fenton. A couple of security guards have been accosted by the haunting scent of lilacs when doing their nightly rounds in the empty building. Is the scent from the ghostly woman on the stairs? There's also the mischievous spirit of a former light tech who likes to play pranks on living workers and the echoes of a disembodied female voice that often fill the darkness of the opera house.

13

LAPEER COUNTY

*We tell stories of the dead as a way of making a sense of the living.
More than just simple urban legends and campfire tales, ghost stories reveal the
contours of our anxieties, the nature of our collective fears and desires, the things
we can't talk about in any other way. The past we're most afraid to speak aloud
of in the bright light of day is the same past that tends to linger in the ghost
stories we whisper in the dark.*

—*Colin Dickey,* Ghostland: An American History in Haunted Places

When the French explorers, fur traders and missionaries first arrived in the Lower Peninsula in the early 1600s, the area now known as Lapeer County was inhabited by the Chippewa (Ojibwa) and Sauk Nations.

On September 10, 1822, Lapeer County was created in the Michigan Territory along with nine other counties. The boundary lines changed several times over the years before taking their present shape.

Lapeer County was uninhabited by white settlers until around 1828, when James Deneen arrived in what is now Almont Township. He was the only inhabitant until 1830, when two settlements separated by a swamp along the Flint River were created. A.N. Hart called his Lapeer, while Jonathan White called his Whitesville. The county government was organized on February 2, 1835. Hart and White each built a courthouse, hoping theirs would be chosen as the official county courthouse. From

1846 to 1853, supervisors went back and forth between the two until the county decided to purchase Hart's, which is still in use today and holds the title of Michigan's oldest working courthouse. White's courthouse was turned into White's Opera House.

The surrounding communities of Almont, Dryden and Imlay City were also founded in the early 1830s. The city of Lapeer is the county seat and is located about twenty miles east of Flint, along the Flint River. The name comes from the French word *la pierre*, which means stone.

OAKDALE: THE LAPEER STATE HOME

Ghost stories are a way of talking about things we're not otherwise allowed to discuss: a forbidden history we thought bricked up safely in the walls.
—*Colin Dickey*

This once idyllic-appearing home for Michigan residents with mental disabilities hid horrific acts of medical violence, forced sterilizations and false imprisonments.

The Michigan Home for the Feeble-Minded and Epileptic opened in June 1895. Over the years, it changed names to the Michigan Home and Training School and the Lapeer State Home and Training School. When it closed in 1991, it was known as Oakdale Regional Center for Development Disabilities.

At one time, a huge portion of Lapeer was taken up by this institution, which sprawled over 1,100 acres and had over 100 buildings. In 1941, the institution's population was larger than the city of Lapeer's by 815 residents. For ninety-four years, it was a major feature of the Lapeer community and economy. Employees took home large paychecks and received excellent health insurance, pensions and paid days off.

But the institution had a darker side no one liked to talk about; in fact, former employees are barred from talking about it due to the nondisclosure agreements they had to sign.

In the late 1800s, mental "defectives" were a burden on poor families and orphanages. Legislators in Lansing passed a bill on June 2, 1893, to build a two-hundred-bed institution. Governor John T. Rich from Elba Township strongly recommended the Lapeer location. The Lapeer Town Council promised to provide 160 acres, a water line to the grounds and free water

Lapeer Home For the Feeble Minded & Epileptic postcard. *Author collection.*

for five years. The state home opened on June 1, 1895, and the first patients were admitted three weeks later. The years passed, and the facility grew. Cottages to house residents and staff were constructed, along with a laundry, nursery, kitchen, barns, silos, school, hospital, butcher shop, bakery, chapel auditorium and garage.

The famous "castle" administration building was the most well-known structure in the facility. In addition to being the administration building, it also housed the superintendent and his family. Castle construction was started in 1901 and completed in 1904. By January 1973, the building had fallen into disrepair and was being used for storage. It became the target of arsonists and was badly damaged. It was torn down in November of that year.

The large chapel auditorium opened in 1904 and seated seven hundred. It was where musicals and plays were put on by the residents. Religious services were also held there. The basement featured a gymnasium and bowling alley for employees to use. The chapel was destroyed by arsonists in April 1939.

At one point, the state home was almost a self-sustaining community. Patients were enrolled in programs to help them "reach their greatest potential." Those capable were taught to read and write, and they were taught arts, textile crafts, woodworking and music. Many learned job skills on the farms, in the bakery and in the sewing room. Some residents of the

Administration Bldg. and Cottages A, B, and C,
Mich. Home F. M. & E., Lapeer, Mich.
Vincent & Son Pub.

Lapeer State Home "The Castle" Postcard. *Author collection.*

facility received job training that allowed them to work off-campus in the Lapeer community.

The home seemed to be a happy place. It held dances, talent shows, movie nights, baseball games and holiday parties that the Lapeer community members were often invited to. Picnicking on the grounds was encouraged.

Yet darkness hid just under the surface.

Rumor has it Building 17 was a place where "difficult" patients were sent. Punishment could consist of solitary confinement, being beaten to submission or something much more sinister. A former employee once told her nephew that there were rooms in the ward rented out by the hour after the Vietnam War. Access to patients who were being punished in Building 17 was included with the room rentals.

Reportedly, many of the residents who lived at the state home did not suffer from any mental or emotional disabilities. Not everyone who was admitted belonged there. A large number of children were dropped off during the Great Depression by parents who couldn't afford to feed or care for them anymore. And according to former employees, some residents were just "overly promiscuous" girls. There were no guidelines for admission. Parents could admit children that "acted up." Men could admit wives who were going through menopause or behaving in ways they didn't like. More than one wrongful imprisonment case was brought

Lapeer State Home and Training School, Lapeer, Mich.

8A-H2786

Lapeer State Home. *Author collection.*

before the courts. At least fifteen patients were set free after being deemed mentally fit to be released.

The home was also involved with eugenics experiments. A Michigan state law passed in 1913 allowed sterilization for "mental defectives" confined to public institutions. The supposed motivation behind the law was to stop unwanted pregnancies at the institutions. It was documented that at least 2,336 patients of the Lapeer home were sterilized against their will, three-fourths of them women. The law included a statement that family had to be notified before the sterilization; unfortunately, most of the people in these institutions had no family, no one to speak up for them. The sterilization law was later declared unconstitutional by a Lapeer circuit court judge and was upheld by the Michigan Supreme Court in 1918. A plaque on the front of the Lapeer Courthouse commemorates that decision. A new law went into effect in 1923 that pertained to "idiots, imbeciles, and feebleminded, but not the insane" that allowed the pro-eugenics crowd to keep sterilizing those in institutions. In 1929, the act was expanded to include "insane and epileptic persons, moral degenerates, and sexual perverts likely to become a menace to society or wards of the state." This practice of forced sterilization didn't end until the 1970s.

It is thought that many experimental and dangerous treatments were used at the state home: electroshock, debilitating medications, psychological manipulation and torture. The home was accused of abuse and wrongful deaths several times. Sadly, most patients didn't have anyone looking out for them. Many were wards of the state with the state or the home acting as their guardian.

The home often made local headlines, usually for financial reasons or the occasional runaway, but there were darker headlines as well, like those about inmate suicides, devastating fires and a fourteen-year-old escapee who went on a robbery spree in Durand.

In 1929, it was murder that made the headlines. Blanche Burke, aged twenty-nine, was the assistant supervisor of the laundry facilities at the Lapeer State Home. On July 26, 1929, she was due to arrive at her in-laws home but never showed. They got worried and made frantic calls searching for her. Finally, they grabbed flashlights and went out in the night. Sadly, they found her body. She had been gagged, bound and dragged off DeMille Road into a wooded area. Her naked body lay on a rock, hands and feet bound behind her back. She was badly bruised with finger marks around her throat. She had been strangled to death. An extensive investigation led police to Lewis Johnson, aged twenty, an inmate of the state home. He worked in the laundry where Blanch Burke had been an assistant supervisor. Apparently, she had chastised him for talking to female patients and threatened to report him. Witnesses say he left immediately after she did that Saturday. Other witnesses placed him in the area where her body had been found. He confessed to the crime and was sent to a prison for the criminally insane. Blanche Burke was buried at Mt. Hope Cemetery.

Another headline crime that shocked locals occurred in October 1949. State home resident Elizabeth Fox was granted a community work release. Her job was in the home of the Merz family. Fox was described as "well-behaved, mild-mannered and shy." But after working in the Merz home for a while, she became upset with how she was being treated by the lady of the house and stabbed Mrs. Merz with a kitchen knife. Fox said she "lost all control" and was sorry she did such a terrible thing. Mrs. Merz survived the stabbing but lost an eye.

Many residents died at the home—some by suicide, some by "natural causes" and some by illness. Many deaths at the home are attributed to the smallpox outbreak of 1910. It was so bad that the facility had to be forcefully quarantined by the Flint National Guard, which camped out on the grounds throughout that autumn and winter to make sure no one left and spread the illness.

A mostly unmarked cemetery remains on the former grounds of the state home. At one time, several graves were marked with stones, but due to time and vandals, not much is left. Records indicate there are close to six hundred residents buried on the grounds, though some say there could be many more residents whose deaths were not properly recorded.

In the 1970s, mental healthcare began to radically change. People were seeing things in a new light and no longer wanted to segregate those who were mentally or physically disabled. Everyone deserved a place in the community. Large state homes were being emptied as residents were sent to adult foster care homes that popped up in subdivisions and rural communities. Adult foster care homes were licensed and regulated by the state and offered accessible features in the setting of a normal home.

Oakdale closed its doors in September 1991. Only four hundred acres and several vacant buildings remained. The state sold everything to the City of Lapeer for one dollar and awarded grants to tear down most of the remaining buildings. Buildings 45, 49 and 71 were saved and repurposed. The old nursery building (45) is now the Lapeer campus of Mott Community College, Building 71 became Chatfield Charter School and Building 49 became Woodside Alternative School. In 2009, it was remodeled and reopened as Rolland-Warner Middle School. A dolphin statue was found during demolition of the state home. It now stands on the Chatfield Charter School grounds. Several ornamental wood and copper cupolas were saved from Buildings 35 and 36 and placed around the city of Lapeer as statement pieces. Lapeer's official city logo now features a cupola.

Numerous paranormal investigators have visited the area where Oakdale once stood. The entire property is considered extremely haunted. It is said to have a strange and spooky vibe to it. Disembodied voices, dark shadows and haunting screams plague the area.

The Mott Campus feels dark and foreboding. Several people who walk their dogs in the area say the dogs will not step foot on the Mott campus.

Chatfield Elementary has numerous tales of ghosts. Children often report seeing nurses in old-fashioned uniforms walking the halls, and teachers who stay late will hear footsteps and voices echoing in empty hallways. Lights can often be seen randomly flickering in the night.

Former Lapeer resident Justin Arnold grew up hearing stories about the institution. He tried to write about Oakdale for his senior project in high school but was forced to pick a different topic. He attended school at the Woodside building before it changed to Rolland-Warner. He always felt that the school had an eerie vibe to it—like you're "never alone, that you're

Chatfield Dolphin found at Oakdale. *Photo by Roxanne Rhoads.*

Chatfield School Lapeer. *Photo by Roxanne Rhoads.*

constantly being watched, patrolled and kept in line." He felt the same at the Mott building. "You always feel like there's a nurse behind you watching every move."

The old cemetery has the most paranormal activity. The cemetery is plagued by screams, moaning, wailing and other strange noises, along with orbs, shadow figures and a horrible feeling of unease that just lingers. One paranormal group captured two disembodied female voices and the sound of footsteps on camera.

A short distance away from the cemetery is a large door that leads to the tunnels of Oakdale—tunnels that are thought to have once spanned the Oakdale property and connected buildings within the facility for easy transport. The City of Lapeer keeps the tunnels tightly locked and uses them for storage. Rumors abound that lost spirits roam the dark tunnels.

BRUCE MANSION (BURNSIDE TOWNSHIP)

The Bruce Mansion is an imposing Second Empire Victorian structure that has been known to stop traffic along M-53. The mansion was built in 1876 and sits on the corner of M-53 (Van Dyke) and Burnside Roads in Burnside Township, Brown City, located in Lapeer County. This beautifully spooky structure just appears out of nowhere and looks like something straight out of a horror movie or a creepy gothic novel.

The property on which the Bruce Mansion sits was originally owned by John C. Emery, who was awarded 160 acres on February 16, 1857, by President Franklin Pierce. The property was sold to J. Gunn in 1863. Gunn sold the farm to John Bruce in 1874.

John Gairns Bruce was born on December 6, 1839, in Kilrenny, Fife, Scotland. In 1855, he moved to the United States with his parents and settled in Almont. He married Jane Webster in 1861. He was a store clerk until 1866, when he opened his store with partner Daniel Webster, his brother-in-law. The business unfortunately burned in November of that year.

Bruce's elaborate mansion was constructed in 1876 along with a new general store on the property. In several stories about the Bruce mansion, John is thought to be a lumber baron, but there were no records found that confirm that. All the records show that John G. Bruce was the Burnside postmaster and a merchant.

The Bruce Mansion. *Photo by Roxanne Rhoads.*

During the Thumb Fire of 1881, the Bruce Mansion was spared while most buildings in the area were destroyed. In February 1883, burglars ravaged Bruce's general store, which was also the post office, and blew the door off the safe, taking all the money and postage stamps. The thieves also stole many other goods from the store. The next day, the goods were found in a shed behind the Presbyterian church. In the book *History of Lapeer*, published in 1884, Bruce is mentioned; it says that he had been postmaster for sixteen years and had "one of the largest and finest residences" in Lapeer County, where he was cultivating his farm of forty acres.

The beautiful architecture made the home a popular event epicenter throughout the years. Many parties and church gatherings happened at the Bruce Mansion. Many funerals also took place in the home, as was common during that time.

The Bruce Mansion hits the Michigan most haunted lists every year, for good reason. Numerous shadow people and ghostly figures have been seen by residents and visitors, and strange sounds have been heard, including growling coming from the basement.

Several occupants have died in the house, including John Bruce's first wife, Jane, in 1885 and his mother, Ann, in 1898. In the early 1900s, Cynthia Smith acquired the home; she passed away in it in 1918. Many articles about the Bruce Mansion list her death as "mysterious" and occurring in 1920 or 1921, but her death certificate states her death happened on February 7, 1918, from bronchial pneumonia. Another story about the mansion mentions a John Walker owning the home in the 1920s; legend says Walker became so distraught when his wife left him in 1925 that he allegedly ran down a pedestrian, buried him in the yard and then hanged himself in the tower. No records confirm this. In fact, John Walker's death certificate shows that he died on April 30, 1929, from endocarditis.

The house changed hands numerous times throughout the twentieth century, eventually ending up with the Kreiner family, which then sold it to Richard and Peggy Tripp. Peggy can't remember what year they bought it and still wonders why they wanted to live in an old mansion that had a general store on the property. No one in her family liked to go up to the third floor; her husband would drag his feet on making repairs, even waiting until he could get their son, Marty, to accompany him. Their time in the home wasn't too spooky, though one night while they were watching *The Amityville Horror*, when the movie got to the scene with the wallpaper cracking and peeling, the same scary sounds started emanating from the Tripp's dining room. They found a strip of wallpaper had peeled away from the wall and was blowing over the hot air register.

In the 1990s, the home ended up in the hands of Barbara Millsap and her brother Bill Masiak. They intended to restore the home and turn it into a bed-and-breakfast. In 1996, Masiak mentioned to the *Lapeer County Press* that he believed the property to be haunted.

In 2009, the Waites acquired the home, intending it to be the perfect location for their costume rental company. They felt the location was extremely haunted and called in investigators, Grimstone Inc. Paranormal Researchers, to substantiate their claims. One of the team members was so distraught by the paranormal activity at the mansion they left the organization. In 2011, Beyond Paranormal was called to investigate. During their investigation, they recorded over two dozen EVPs, one member was pushed by unseen hands and one video camera suddenly toppled over as it captured the voice of a small child saying "Grandpa." The Waites closed their rental company.

The house is currently owned by Tad and Claudia Leake, who purchased the home in January 2019, and at the time of this writing, they are working hard to restore the home to its original glory.

Investigators, visitors and the Leakes have spotted numerous ghosts, including a woman with a long neck, a young girl, a bearded man and other apparitions, including a cat. Growls can be heard coming from the basement. Most recently, large black masses appeared in photos of the house during a paranormal investigation. In May 2021, a Quinceañera photo shoot took place in the mansion. When the photographer was going over the young woman's photos, she discovered the beautiful fifteen-year-old's face had been replaced by that of a creepy old man.

The building is private property; please respect that. After months of problems with curious people trespassing despite the "No Trespassing" signs and numerous cameras on the property, the Leakes opened their home to the curious for tours and investigations in the summer of 2021. As of this writing, they have stopped tours to return their focus on restorations. Please connect with the owners of the Bruce Mansion if you are interested in visiting; they can be found on Facebook.

CASTAWAYS FOOD AND SPIRITS

Nestled at the end of a dead-end road lies a property that once featured a bustling resort, a hotel, a popular bar and finally an upscale restaurant. Now all that remains is a decrepit husk, a cracked parking lot and a spectacular view of Lake Nepessing.

The location started life as Hunt's Landing, one of three popular locations that brought tourists to Lake Nepessing in the late 1800s. Joseph Hunt built the *Belle of the Lake*, a sixty-foot boat with two decks that could hold three hundred people. It was quite the draw. Over the years, Hunt's Landing added the Lake Nepessing Hotel, twenty-two cottages and a large house for the boat's captain.

After World War II, "The Hotel" was a bar where young adults congregated to drink and dance the night away to live music. Before her death in 2018, Doris Burke authored the *County Press* column Lapeer Memories, in which she would often recount her early life in the 1940s. She mentioned the hotel several times as a hot spot where she and her friends would hang out.

After several fires, the old hotel finally closed its doors for good in 1983. In 1991, new owners decided to turn it into an upscale restaurant. It had several names over the years, including Gilligan's and the Pelican.

Now all that remains on what should be prime real estate is an abandoned eyesore bearing no resemblance to the bustling hub it once was. The land gives off a feeling of menace like it doesn't want anyone or anything to

All that is left of Castaways. *Photo by Roxanne Rhoads.*

disturb it. Most of the buildings and landmarks, like the lighthouse, were torn down in June 2020. Why? No one seems to know. Were there plans to build something new? Were the plans put off because of COVID?

Could the location be cursed? Is it the ghosts that keep people away?

While the restaurant was open, there were many reports of patrons and employees hearing voices near the restrooms, feeling cold hands around their necks when they were near the roof staircase, seeing objects move by themselves and hearing voices in the shadows telling them to leave immediately.

The Magick Man Justin Arnold talked to staff years ago about the spirits. He said almost everyone who worked there had a story to tell. Waitstaff told tales of customers that vanished into thin air. A chef would see people in the kitchen out of the corner of their eye only to turn and find no one there. Staff would often hear voices outside when they were closing up for the night, voices that never seemed to have bodies attached to them.

Witnesses have seen the apparition of a man sitting on the dock and walking off the dock into the lake and a ghostly woman near and on the lighthouse that once stood on the property. She was often spotted at the top of the lighthouse leaning over the platform. People have also seen human shapes out on the lake with no rippling effect. Kathleen Stroman, who was a partial owner of Castaways, attests that the location was definitely haunted. The staff named one ghost Sam, stating that giving it a name made it less scary.

Angela L., a local who lives by the old restaurant, says that the entire hill is haunted: "My house, all the houses up the hill have spirit activity."

Could there be something in the history that could explain the ghostly activity? There are rumors a firefighter died during a fire at the hotel, but that story could not be confirmed, nor were any other deaths on the property discovered.

Perhaps the lake itself holds answers. Lake Nepessing is dense with weeds that people can get tangled in, and it gets cold toward the bottom of the lake, averaging about fifty degrees. But it is such a small lake there have not been many fatalities. In the 1970s, two snowmobiles broke through the ice, and one man drowned; in 1980, three people died in a plane crash. In August 2009, the body of local doctor Antoun Aftimos was found two hundred yards offshore of the Castaways restaurant. He had been swimming with his family when he slipped underwater and disappeared. It took three days to find the body.

Past Tense Country Store, Arts and Antiques, Cider Mill and After Dark Haunt Attraction

The Past Tense empire started life as the Farnsworth Farm on the corner of Farnsworth and Daley Roads in Lapeer, Michigan. Rumored to be a stop on the Underground Railroad, the location is full of history; one building is original to the farm and dates to the 1840s. Many people feel the energy is quite eerie. Whispers of ghostly encounters and strange happenings haunt the location but never deter from the welcome and open vibe of the store.

Farnsworth Road is named after Christopher Farnsworth, who resided in Mayfield Township. Farnsworth was born to Asa and Mimi Farnsworth on December 25, 1814, in Westminster, Massachusetts. He married Malissa P. Glidden on July 15, 1846. His family was one of four original settlers in Lapeer. Over the years, he had many roles as a township official, including notary public and highway commissioner.

Rumor says he's buried on the Past Tense property, where he wanted to face his farm for all eternity—at least that's the story Neil Lechner, the grandson of Past Tense store owners, used when he first created the haunt attractions at Past Tense in 2009. It's not surprising that real haunted locations often get turned into Halloween attractions. It's fun to play off tales from history to create a back story for your Halloween haunt. A listing on FamilySearch. org indicates Farnsworth died on March 4, 1888, but there are no official records containing his burial location.

Lechner's grandparents Chuck and Lucie Hiner opened the store in 1971.

In August 2011, they suffered a devastating fire that "took seven fire departments nearly seven hours to bring under control." The fire caused around $1.1 million in damages, destroying about two-thirds of their retail space, but the Hiners remained open and rebuilt making the store better than ever. Sadly, in May 2019, Lucille "Lucie" Rhadigan Hiner passed away after a long illness.

The store and haunted attractions remain open, a staple of the Lapeer area. The top window of the barn turned store originally had a window with a pentacle built into it. The pentagram or five-pointed star is a symbol of protection. Local Wiccan Justin Arnold feels that the location is welcoming and comforting: "Being a witch, this place has always lent its energy to those who need it."

The history of the location continues to play out in this time for those sensitive enough to see. Sometimes you can drive by the apple orchards and spot ghostly workers tending to the trees, a job now done by machinery.

The White Horse Inn (Metamora)

Lorenzo Hoard and his wife, Lucy Carpenter Hoard, moved from New York to Metamora in 1850 and purchased a general store. They remodeled it and named it Hoard House, an inn and stagecoach stop. Rumors say it also became a stop on the Underground Railroad and was included in the book *Hauntings of the Underground Railroad: Ghosts of the Midwest*.

When the Michigan Central Railroad came through Metamora in 1872, the inn became a popular place for train passengers to stay for fifty cents a night. In the 1876 Atlas of Lapeer County, Hoard House was noted for having "good accommodations for travelers, feed and stabling for horses."

The White Horse Inn. *Courtesy of the White Horse Inn and Jacob Hawkins Photography.*

In 1905, William Deter and August Miller of the Deter House purchased Hoard House. During the Prohibition era, owner Frank Peters changed the name to the White Horse. Over the years, the White Horse passed through numerous hands. It has been a dance hall, boarding house, bar, ice cream parlor and restaurant.

Drawn to its history and its future possibilities, Tim and Lisa Wilkins purchased the White Horse in 2001. In 2012, they made the difficult decision to close because it needed too many costly renovations. At the time, it held the state title for the longest continuously operating restaurant.

Victor Dzenowagis and his wife, Linda Egeland, purchased the restaurant, knowing the village of Metamora needed the White Horse. They did extensive renovations and reopened in 2014. Over $3 million went into reviving the White Horse. The result is exquisite.

Craftsmen, architects, stonemasons, farmers, businesses and an artist from France, all contributed their skills and resources to help create something unique and beautiful. The dining room floor was created by Metamora resident John Yarema, made with wood from thirty-five cherry, red mapl, and white oak trees taken from the grounds of Dzenowagis and Egeland's eighty-acre farm in Metamora. The wood was milled by a fifth-generation sawyer in Lapeer. The main dining room chandeliers are antique hay hooks from a nearby 1880s barn. Stones from the same barn are now the inn's massive fireplace and chimney, which were constructed by members of the local Giddings family, who have been stonemasons for at least three

White Horse fireplace.
Courtesy of the White Horse Inn and Michael Kramer.

generations. The fireplace mantel is a beam from the same barn. French artist Jean Louis Sauvat added the large charcoal horses on the wall of the main dining room.

The couple restored the original structure that belonged to Lorenzo Hoard but tore down many of the additions that had been added over the years. They added a large side patio overlooking a staging area for carriage and sleigh rides, an elevator, new upstairs bathrooms, a balcony and a much larger kitchen.

Lorenzo Hoard died in 1888, but it seems he never left. Many think Lorenzo has stayed on to be the caretaker and protector of the old inn.

Owner Linda Egeland, a former chemist who never believed in the supernatural, thinks Lorenzo is still around. She even said in a 2014 *Detroit*

Top: The White Horse Inn horses and wood floor. *Courtesy of the White Horse Inn and Michael Kramer.*

Bottom: Hoard House historical marker. *Photo by Roxanne Rhoads.*

Free Press interview that "our manager, Chris, was in the basement and took a picture there…with a ghost standing in it. It looks like a guy in suspenders. It looks like a farmer."

The old building has many unexplained cold spots, creepy creaking stairs, slamming doors, ghostly footsteps and flickering lights—all with no human source. Staff members often feel like they are being watched even when no one is around. A current staff member at the White Horse is terrified to close at night. The building is so spooky, he never wants to be alone in the place.

A legend claims that several men and a barmaid were killed in a fire in the front section of the bar. Guests have sworn they heard screams and moaning in that area—could it be from those who perished in the fire?

South East Michigan Ghost Hunters investigated the White Horse, and one of their team reported seeing a young male watching the inn's staff. They caught quite a bit of activity, including some orbs on film. Paranormal investigators are divided on orbs. Some swear they are nothing more than dust and light, while others are adamant that orbs are otherworldly energy. Roxanne visited the White Horse for a delightful dinner, and there wasn't an orb in sight. The only spooky thing she experienced was a couple of unexplained cold spots.

Over the years, many apparitions have been seen on the premises, including those of what appear to be escaped slaves, a man dressed in a 1940s-style tuxedo, a young girl and an old man.

The William Peter Mansion (Columbiaville)

William Peter was born in Germany in the early 1800s. He made his way to the United States by stowing away on a ship. He arrived in New York and worked in the lumber industry. By the 1850s, he had become a millionaire with his hands in a little bit of everything, including lumber, banking and farming. In 1852, he married Roxana Clute when she was just seventeen. Her father did not approve, so they eloped and settled in Toledo, Ohio, where their two children, Harriet and Alvin, were born.

They returned to Columbiaville, where Peter built much of the town, platting it in 1871. From 1879 to 1899, he built a gristmill, a woolen mill, a school, a church and many other businesses along with houses for his workers.

In 1892, the Peters decided to build their retirement home. William Peter picked a site right in the middle of town on the corner of Second and Water

Streets. The majority of the layout and design for the beautiful Italianate was done by Roxana. Many of the materials used in the mansion's construction came from Peter's own companies. The wood was shipped from the Peter factories in Toledo and Bay City. The brick was from the Peter brickyard. The only materials that did not come from Peter's operations were the marble, sinks and tubs, which came from Europe.

The Peter family moved into the sixteen-room mansion in 1896. Unfortunately, William Peter didn't get to enjoy it for long. He passed away in 1899. Roxana lived in the mansion until she passed away in 1917.

The Lapeer County Historical Society placed a historical marker on the lawn in 1972. The mansion was registered with the National Register of Historic Places in 1979.

In the 1980s, the Mansion was owned by the State of Michigan and turned into low-income housing. In the 1990s, the mansion sat empty until 1998, when Teresa Cook caught a glimpse of the interior through an open doorway during a yard sale By September 1998, she had the keys to the mansion and, with help from her family, began restoring it to its original glory.

The building has been a bed-and-breakfast for years.

Before COVID, the William Peter Mansion often opened its doors for ghost hunts, murder mystery dinners and other fun events like a Witches Ball during the Halloween season. Unfortunately, with COVID many events were canceled. The mansion went up for sale in July 2021. After months on the market, it still had not sold. Maybe the ghosts are scaring people away.

HauntedJourneys.com describes the mansion as one of the most haunted places in Michigan. On National Ghost Hunting Day 2018, the William Peter Mansion was one of 150 sites around the world to participate in the search for spirits as part of the World's Largest Ghost Hunt. Two teams of paranormal experts led guests on an investigation in the house.

The main staircase leading to the second floor is a haunt hot spot. Many have seen the ghost of a woman dressed in Victorian clothing. The bed-and-breakfast's website even showcases a photo of the phantom on the stairs. Over the years, many guests have reported hearing whispers and seeing doors open and close on their own. Some people have heard footsteps when they knew no one else is in the building. EVP have been recorded in the attic, sometimes accompanied by unexplained knocking. Groans and moans have also been captured on digital recordings. One investigation captured the voice of a little girl in the attic. A team of investigators thinks there are at least five separate spirits in the old mansion, including one whose name is Lucy.

14
Urban Legends and Oddities

The Michigan Dogman and Loup-Garou

He was beloved by all, and most of all by the children;
For he told them tales of the Loup-garou in the forest,
And of the goblin that came in the night to water the horses,
And of the white Létiche, the ghost of a child who unchristened Died,
and was doomed to haunt unseen the chambers of children;

—Henry Wadsworth Longfellow, Evangeline

The Dogman is a popular cryptozoological creature in Michigan. Some say it has had more sightings than Bigfoot. The first reported sighting in Michigan happened in 1887 in Wexford County. Two lumberjacks were in the woods when they spotted an odd creature with the body of a man and the head of a dog.

In 1930, Robert Fortney was fishing on the Muskegon River near Paris, Michigan, when a pack of wild dogs came crashing out of the woods. Fortney fired his gun, scaring them off, except for one, a massive black dog that stood up on its hind legs and stared Fortney down with terrifying blue eyes. Fortney shot again, and the creature ran off into the forest on two legs.

The creature is most often described as a six- to seven-foot-tall bipedal canine-like animal with the torso of a man, the head of a wolf and a terrifying scream-like howl. Those who have seen the Dogman detail a furry beast with pointed ears and a large muzzle. It is often spotted on the side of a road near a dark wooded area, chowing down on roadkill or whatever animal it happened to kill.

The part that tends to scare the hell out of anyone who happens to see the Dogman is when it stands up and you catch a glimpse of razor-sharp fangs and bright eyes reflecting a blaze of amber or blue. Then there's the fact it often runs away incredibly fast on two legs.

French settlers came to Michigan with tales of the Loup Garou (pronounced loo garoo), which is French for "werewolf." These tales can be traced back to the 1700s in Michigan, especially around large settlements like Detroit. But werewolves transform from man to beast and back to a man.

The Dogman is different. "It's fully canine, walks on its hind legs, uses its forelimbs to carry chunks of…roadkill or deer carcasses," said author Linda S. Godfrey. "They have pointed ears on top of their heads. They have big fangs. They have bushy tails. They walk—most tellingly—digitigrade, or on their toe pads, as all canines do, and that's something that a human in a fur suit really can't duplicate," Linda wrote in an article published by the *Huffington Post* in 2012.

Godfrey is an author who has been researching the Dogman since 1991. She told the *Huffington Post* that the area around Kalamazoo and the Manistee National Forest are hot spots for Michigan creature sightings.

Godfrey hadn't caught a glimpse of one until the summer of 2006, when she spotted one just north of Reed City, Michigan. She was with the videographer of the History Channel's *MonsterQuest* shooting for the episode "American Werewolf." There had been numerous sightings of the Michigan Dogman in that location. They were on the hunt, and after hours of not seeing much, suddenly something gray, furry and around six feet tall ran across the gravel road around 1:00 a.m. on that hot July night.

Tales of the Dogman gained strength in the twentieth century when disc jockey Steve Cook at WTCM-FM in Traverse City, Michigan, recorded a song titled "The Legend," which he initially played as an April Fool's Day joke in 1987. He has claimed that the story was just a joke and he knew nothing about Dogman reports before the song aired. The song is still often played throughout Michigan during the Halloween season.

> *Somewhere in the north-woods darkness, a creature walks upright. And the best advice you may ever get is never to go out…at night.*
> —*"The Legend" by Steve Cook*

Soon after the song first aired, reports of sightings started coming into Cook's radio station. Since then, people from all over Michigan have reported seeing a Dogman. But where did the Dogman come from?

One legend declares that the Dogman appears to humans in a ten-year cycle that falls on years ending in the number seven. Other versions of the story claim it appears in seven-year cycles.

Cook has now done extensive research on Dogman sightings and stories. In a 2012 *Huffington Post* article, he revealed that he once "spoke with an elder from the Ottawa-Chippewa tribe in the 1980s who believed dogmen were members of a shapeshifting skinwalker tribe who became stuck somewhere between their human and animal forms." "There was this warlike tribe and they had the ability to transform themselves into any creature they chose when going into battle," Cook said. "They chose the wolf because he was the scariest and the most awesome." What the tribe probably did, he said, is cover themselves in wolf pelts when preparing to fight.

In 2006, Linda S. Godfrey received a letter from David Walks As Bear— former Michigan game warden, author and member of the Shawnee Nation. It said:

> *Shapeshifters are usually considered as good, a tad mischievous maybe, but not evil. The same can't be said for their opposite skinwalkers, eh. If the Michigan Dog Men are shapeshifters, then they'd be spooky, alright, as they're other-worldly. But not evil, though. So it could be that the Dog Men of Michigan are just old Michigan Indian warriors, going through their seven-year routine of shape shifting. Who can say? But speaking of routine I do personally fret a bit when I'm driving deep in the dark woods; on a full-mooned night and things change know what I mean?*

Godfrey thinks the Dogman and other beasts are spirit creatures from another world; they come here and assume corporeal form, then return to the spirit world. In Godfrey's book *The Michigan Dogman*, she recounts numerous sightings throughout Michigan, mostly in the upper part of the mitten and in the UP. Sightings in the northern areas include Traverse City, Manistee, Muskegon County and Ludington. To the south, there have been sightings in Holly, Oxford, Rochester, DeWitt, Ann Arbor, Sturgis, Portage, Hickory Corners and Battle Creek.

A high number of sightings seem to occur near liminal spaces such as bridges, crossroads and highway entry and exit ramps and close to graveyards, burial mounds and other areas often associated with supernatural energy.

According to Nick Redfern of MysteriousUniverse.org,

> *There is distinct high-strangeness attached to such reports, too, including the locations: bridges, crossroads, and so on. Of course, any student of folklore will be aware that such locations have, for centuries, been associated with fantastic beasts and paranormal phenomena. Plus, Linda cites in her writings a number of reports where these creatures have been seen near to entrance and exit roads to highways—which is surely an upgrading of the old crossroads motif in such cases. There are other locations that play a role in such cases, too: graveyards, ancient burial mounds, effigy sites, and more.*

In 2007, a video known as the "Gable film"—which claimed to have captured images of a Dogman—began to circulate on the internet. The video was later revealed to be a hoax on the History Channel's *MonsterQuest*.

Roxanne remembers hearing the song and scary tales about the Dogman as a child. Most were just stories told around campfires or during the Halloween season, but there were nights she was terrified to go near a window for fear of seeing a monster with a canine head staring at her. Her hometown of Flint has had its share of weird wolf tales and Dogman sightings.

The *Great Lakes Pilot* published a story detailing Earl Eastman's November 1935 encounter with an abnormally large wolf. Eastman was a deer hunter from Flint who shot a wolf that was going after a deer near the Rhody Creek Trail, which is between Sweeney and Grand Marais. The wolf was huge. It weighed 182 pounds after being gutted. Earl brought the wolf back to Flint, where it ended up on display in a barbershop for two years. It was later taken to the Carnegie Institute in Pittsburgh and put on display. The wolf was officially measured at seven feet, eleven inches long, thirty-nine inches at the shoulders and twelve and three-quarters inches across the skull. According to a blog, *Life at Random*, on contacting the Carnegie Institute about the wolf, the institute claimed that it was lost. In fact, curators cannot find any records of it and have no idea where it went. Was this just an abnormally large wolf or something else? Loup Garou? Dogman?

A man on the message board Unexplained Mysteries claimed to have encountered the Dogman in Flint in 1973:

> *I was a teenager; I was staying with my Uncle Jay and Aunt Shell in the summer of 1973. I was between my sophomore and junior years in high school. My Uncle drove a local grocery delivery truck…in the Flint Michigan area. Well, late on a Thursday night (about 11:30), we were*

headed up the winding road that snaked around the hill up to the truck park, and we both saw what we thought was a big dog on the side of the road, pawing at something. As we got closer, I saw the thing was rooting and licking something with tongue and snout. Then the SOB stood up. This was no dog! My Uncle slowed to a crawl (not quite stopping) and hit the high beams, and what I saw scared me so bad that I couldn't even get a scream out! It was a MAN, covered in short, black fur, clearly well-muscled with the head of a German Shepherd or wolf. I could hardly breathe. Its eyes were yellow-orange colored....We didn't make a sound but started to roll by, when it lunged across the access road in a single leap.

Black Panther Sightings

A 140-pound black cat is not what you'd expect to see strolling the streets of Flint, but numerous people have claimed to see just that. Tales of black panthers in the Flint area date to the mid-1980s.

On August 13, 1984, three employees at the Fisher Body Plant witnessed a large cat around 8:30 a.m. in the alley across from the factory. The *Flint Journal* reported four other sightings of a black panther in Flint's suburbs that same day. On December 3, 1984, a truck driver in Flint claimed to have almost run over a panther at 6:30 a.m. He told the *Flint Journal* the cat stopped and looked at him before scurrying off into the darkness. Also in 1984, a male black panther weighing around 140 pounds was shot at by two teenagers using a 12-gauge shotgun loaded with birdshot.

Mysterious panther sightings are quite common in Michigan; in fact, black panther sightings are quite popular all over the United States. Some equate them to being the four-legged version of Bigfoot sightings.

Panther is a blanket term for many big cats. An actual black panther is a melanistic jaguar or leopard. When you look closely at their fur, you can see the spots in the black coat. Jaguars and leopards are not native to the United States. And they are not what people describe in their black panther sightings; what they describe is a puma concolor (aka the cougar, mountain lion, catamount and painter). A cougar generally occurs in tawny-red and slate-gray color forms.

The problem with seeing a black one is that they don't exist. Not a single scientifically confirmed or preserved specimen has ever been known to exist.

However, cryptozoologist Dr. Karl Shuker, author of *Mystery Cats of the World*, mentions on his website,

In 1843, a bona fide black puma was shot in the Carandahy River section of Brazil by professional hunter William Thomson, but regrettably its skin was not retained. In addition, I have seen various online mentions of an enigmatic taxiderm cat dubbed the "Cherokee cougar" that has been claimed to be a black puma. Measuring 6 ft 2 in (1.87 m) long, and variously said to have been shot in Tennessee or Montana, it has been denounced by skeptics as a normal puma that has been dyed black, or some entirely different feline species. However, hair samples from it that were tested by researchers from the zoology department of East Tennessee State University confirmed that they had not been dyed, and DNA samples verified that it was a puma. Nevertheless, photos of it (not seen by me so far) apparently suggest that it is dark brown rather than truly black.

In December 2020, *National Geographic* posted about a white cougar sighting. "Taken in 2013, the photographs were the first confirmed case of a wild cougar with leucism, a genetic mutation that turns most of its body white." "That shows you how extremely unusual it is," said Luke Hunter, executive director of the Wildlife Conservation Society's Big Cats Program and author of the book *Wild Cats of the World*. "It's a striking set of photos. Genetic color aberrations, such as albinism and leucism, are relatively common among wild cats, but for unknown reasons, they're almost unheard of in cougars, a successful predator whose habitat stretches from Canada to Chile, the biggest north-south range of any "wild cat."

So black cougars could exist. Melanism, a surplus of the black pigment melanin, is a genetic mutation just like albinism and leucism. Melanism is recessive in leopards and dominant in jaguars. It is known to occur in fourteen of the forty wild cat species. There are two recorded instances of albinism in cougars and now two recorded instances of leucism. No known cases of melanism have ever been found in cougars. That does not mean it is not possible.

So where did Michigan's big black cats come from?

In the book *Weird Michigan* by Linda S. Godfrey, she tells a tale of "black panthers" from the Forest of Doom. The Forest of Doom is also known as Gogomain Swamp, which is twenty-five miles south of Sault Ste. Marie. The forest is so thick there that it is thirty degrees hotter inside the forest than it is outside. Supposedly, this is where Michigan's Mystery Cat comes from. Reports of these mystery cats started in Munuscong Bay in 1954.

But it was the mid-1980s when reports of black panther sightings were happening all over the state. In addition to the 1984 Flint sightings, there were also reports from Manchester, Wixom and Coloma. In 1986, a panther was reported to have killed a prized palomino quarter horse in Milford. A cat hunt was on, with reports of police and federal wildlife officers having seen the cat but unable to capture it. In February 1990, a family in Camden caught the panther on video as it prowled their property. In October 1990, there were two sightings near Muskegon.

Roxanne heard many stories about panthers in the Flint area in the late '80s and early '90s. One rumor was that there was a breeder in Montrose and the panthers kept getting loose. When she was driving down Linden Road one dusky evening in the mid-'90s, something large and black ran through the field next to her. She was alone and caught just a glimpse of a large dark shape darting through the field. It disappeared into the woods. Was it one of the fabled panthers? Maybe. Or it could have been a large dog or even a deer that simply looked black in the fading light.

For a long time, things were quiet, but in 2012, panthers popped up again. The website Cryptomundo reported, "A large feline spotted Sunday, March 31, 2012, near Grand Court Adrian has been identified by a law enforcement official as a black panther. Trooper Sean Street from the Monroe post of the Michigan State Police responded at 5:51 p.m. to a report of a large feline walking in the field."

In September 2012, the Flint Police Operations Facebook page posted

ANIMAL COMPLAINT: Lahring and Linden. Look for a very large cat, looked like a panther.

Black panther sightings started popping up again in the Flint/Flushing area in 2021. In early 2021, a truck driver reported seeing a black panther cross the I-75 freeway somewhere between the Pierson and Mt. Morris Road overpasses. In the Flushing residents group on Facebook, one person reported seeing a black panther along the Flint River in the Flushing area, and another person spotted one in their backyard. In June 2021, Roxanne personally saw a public video posted on Snapchat of a cougar walking around in Flushing, possibly in one of the parks. It was quite clearly a cougar; that long, thick tail is unmistakable. On several occasions in May and June 2021, her youngest son attended bonfires with friends in Flushing, and they heard the frightening sounds from at least one, quite possibly two, cougars prowling the wooded area near the bonfires. A cougar scream is spine-chilling.

While no one has caught a black panther on camera, the DNR has been contacted about the multiple cougar sightings in the Flushing area. Cougars, also known as mountain lions, were originally native to Michigan but were hunted to extinction in the early twentieth century. In the late 2000s, sightings of cougars became so frequent the DNR finally created a cougar team in 2008 to verify and track cougar reports (after years of telling everyone there were no cougars in Michigan). So far, all but one official "confirmed" cougar sighting have been in Michigan's Upper Peninsula.

However, the sheer number of recent sightings in Flushing has people worried and curious.

Melanistic animals are rarer than albinos. If there were melanistic cougars in this area decades ago and they bred with regular cougars, the genetic abnormality could have passed on to show up generations later, which could be why we didn't see them for a couple of decades. Genetic mutations can occur through inbreeding. In an area that supposedly doesn't even have cougars, the probability of inbreeding is pretty high—therefore increasing the possibility of genetic mutations. So, in theory, it is possible a melanistic cougar (black panther) could be prowling the area.

The Creepy Clowns of 2016

In the fall of 2016, weird stories of clown sightings swept the country. Bizarre encounters and creepy clowns were reported in at least twenty states and over twenty Michigan cities.

Flint had numerous clown sightings.

What started this crazy clown craze? Was it a promotional stunt for a movie? Perhaps marketing for a haunted Halloween attraction?

No one knows.

The earliest clown sighting was recorded in August 2016 in South Carolina. The *New York Times* reported that children were terrified of clowns trying to lure them into the dark depths of the forest. The sheriff's department in Greenville County, South Carolina, confirmed that several adults and children in an apartment complex next to a wooded area said they had been terrorized by people in clown makeup. They were so scared that some residents fired shots into the woods.

For the next couple of months, clown sightings were popping up everywhere. By early October, the clowns had made their way to Michigan.

Some of the incidents were serious. A Walgreens in Brownstown Township was robbed by an armed clown.

In Sterling Heights, a young boy claimed to be cut by a knife-wielding clown. The boy was not seriously hurt, and the police did not confirm if a clown was involved.

Clown threats forced a Muskegon school into lockdown.

In Roseville, two eighteen-year-old women were arrested after chasing two fourteen-year-old girls while wearing clown masks. They were charged with disorderly conduct.

A clown-masked criminal robbed a hotel in Livonia. Another masked villain robbed a business in Brownstown Township and two businesses in Ann Arbor.

October 3–7, 2016 was the time frame for Flint's most reported clown sightings. Numerous calls to 911 had people panicking.

On October 4, the Mt. Morris Police Department issued a statement on its Facebook page:

> *Mt Morris City Police Department*
> *October 4, 2016 ·*
> *Regarding the clown post aimed at Mt Morris and Beecher Schools…the post has been traced back to a former student playing a prank. There is no cause for concern at this time. Should anyone see something or someone of a suspicious nature don't hesitate to report it to 911 so a car can be dispatched to check it out.*

Here are some of the 911 calls from the Flint/Genesee County area:

> *October 5, 2016 ·*
> *#FLINT #POLICE*
> *SUSPICIOUS—Walton and Brown—Caller says there is a clown with a black and white face standing at the corner.*

> *October 5, 2016 · Flint, MI*
> *Flint—Walton and Brown*
> *Suspicious. Caller said she seen a clown.*

> *October 5, 2016 ·*
> *#MTMORRISTWP #POLICE*
> *SUSPICIOUS—(?) Blk of Neff Rd—Near the woods by (?) elementary. Caller's son said he just seen a clown near the woods.*

October 5, 2016 ·
#VIENNATWP #POLICE
SUSPICIOUS—E side of Linden Rd near (inaudible) caller seen a clown standing by the corn field.

October 5, 2016 ·
#FLINT #POLICE
SUSPICIOUS—address inaudible—Clown walking in the parking lot behind the church. It has been there for about 15 minutes.

October 6, 2016 ·
Flint- 800 blk Moore
SUSPICIOUS, caller's 6 year old son said he seen a clown outside.

October 7, 2016 ·
#FLINT #POLICE
TROUBLE—(?) Blk of 12th St—South Western Academy—13 y/o F student called her mom and said clowns were chasing the students and no one is being allowed in the auditorium, F is having a panic attack. PD is on scene and have been there since earlier this morning and is advising he is not seeing or hearing anything going on and that he has checked with the principal and they are not aware of anything going on either. Caller would like to speak with PD.

On October 6, the Flushing Community School District had to issue a letter to parents:

As you may have seen on both local and national news in the last couple of days, a number of communities across the country are dealing with rumors circulating on social media that are related to "clowns" making vague threats to students and/or school communities. We have been made aware of one incident involving a Flushing student, and while the threat was not found to be credible, we are continuing to work with the Flushing Township Police Department to investigate it thoroughly. We have received calls from a handful of concerned parents throughout the day as false rumors of lockdowns or threats spread. I can assure you that student safety is our first priority, and that there has not been any reason to have our buildings in lockdown today.

After similar events occurred in the Boston area in the 1980s, Loren Coleman, a cryptozoologist, came up with something called "The Phantom Clown Theory." This theory attributes the clown sightings to mass hysteria. But why would clowns spark mass hysteria?

Rami Nader is a Canadian psychologist who studies coulrophobia—the irrational fear of clowns. He believes clown phobias are "fueled by the fact that clowns wear makeup and disguises that hide their true identities and feelings."

Fear of clowns is certainly nothing new, nor is the evil clown trope.

Bad Clowns, by Benjamin Radford, traces how clowns evolved throughout history into unpredictable, menacing creatures. In the 1970s, the connection between clowns and psychopathic killers was pushed into the collective consciousness of Americans thanks to the serial killer John Wayne Gacy, who used to dress up as Pogo the Clown for children's birthday parties.

Authors, television shows and moviemakers continue to play into our clown fears with books, shows and movies such as Stephen King's *It*. Season 7 of *American Horror Story* was possibly inspired by the 2016 clown epidemic—it was even set in Michigan.

Were the creepy clown sightings simply a distraction during the emotional election season of 2016? Or was something more sinister going on?

CAPTAIN BUBBLEGUM

Legend has it that a mythical villain named Captain Bubblegum once stalked Flint's Northside. He was often seen in the wooded Forest Park, now called Max Brandon Park, terrorizing little children. The *Flint Expatriates* blog posted several times about Captain Bubblegum and encouraged readers to write in about their experiences. Numerous people shared their stories of a man wearing a superhero cape riding a moped and terrorizing them on the north side of Flint throughout the '80s and '90s. Sometimes he had bubblegum wrappers stuck to his costume. One person said he had tons of keys and would tell kids he had the key to their house and could come in anytime.

Würstside Warlord wrote:

> *I first became aware of Capt. Bubblegum sometime during the early 80s while attending Walker School (or was it Walker Learning Center?) One morning as the buses arrived from all over the city, the kids who arrived on*

bus #212 from the northwest side were terrified. Scared silly. Hysterical. They reported that a man wearing a superhero outfit had chased them. If memory serves me he struck at both Pierson and Selby. After our teacher interrogated the students it turned out that others had experienced run-ins with this character before....This superhero gone bad was a well-known freakazoid on the north side. Allegedly he never actually caught his prey, but if he did would we ever really know?

MadeMommy also commented on the *Flint Expatriates* post:

He was absolutely real. He stalked me and my sister back in 1985 to 1990. Still traumatized. He was a sick pervert. He had Bubblegum wrappers attached to his jumpsuit and he used to follow, chase and even worse things. I'll never forget his tail. Not a legend it's real. Born and raised in Flint for 18 years. He started stalking me on Wisner which off Pierson and Clio Rd and then in Civic Park neighborhood Humboldt street.

No one's heard from him in years. Who was he and why did he terrorize children? In 2014, Flint twins Dameicko and Tameicko Smith took Flint's urban legend and made it into the horror film *Captain Bubblegum*. The movie can be found on YouTube.

THE MYSTERY OF THE TYRONE SUNKEN GARDENS

The Tyrone Sunken Gardens are a hidden gem tucked behind the Tyrone Memory Gardens Cemetery on White Lake Road outside the Fenton area in Tyrone Township near the border of Genesee and Livingston Counties. If you didn't know it is there, you'd never find it. Old photos show a sign did exist, but it is long gone. At Roxanne's last visit, there was no sign pointing to it, no indication that it is hiding down a hill and into a wooded area outside the cemetery. Now you must look for the statue of a kneeling figure, which has a mystical presence. It makes you feel like he's accepting a quest, a quest that you too can accept. Just follow the path next to him, and it will lead you into a beautiful wooded area down to a babbling brook and a quaint bridge that you must cross to get into the garden.

And you never know what you will find when you get to the garden. Sometimes it is mowed and taken care of; other times it is wild and overgrown, a wet and mushy swampland. One thing is for sure, it will pique your curiosity. It's a strange place, a garden of granite and stone built by a man more mysterious than the place he created.

Charles "Chas" Eugene Smith conceived the idea of the sunken garden while traveling the world. He figured he could create his own beautiful spot in Tyrone Township, something as beautiful and unique as the sunken gardens he had viewed in Australia, Canada, England and New Zealand. He created the park in 1935. He wheeled in loads of sand by hand with a wheelbarrow to create a solid surface for his creation in the soggy marshland.

If you can visit when it is mowed and well taken care of, the full vision is quite awe-inspiring. The stones create a circle around a small white obelisk in the middle that, some say, resembles an altar.

Smith originally placed a sundial in the middle of the large stone, but someone stole the dial. To the east and west, he put welcoming gates. Originally, each gate had a bell; those were stolen as well. In recent years, at least one bell and the sundial have been returned, but they had not been installed at the time of this writing.

Smith laid out walkways like the spokes of a wagon wheel. There are stones for each of the states. Outside the circle are pillars, relics that were once

Entrance to Tyrone Sunken Gardens. *Photo by Roxanne Rhoads.*

hitching posts in Maine, Vermont and New Hampshire—the oldest dates to 1790 and stood along the Mohawk Trail. There's also a huge granite cube with sunburst radials on top. The radials give the distance to foreign cities, cities Smith visited in his travels. Smith circled the globe four times. The poetry etched into the gates is something Smith just "conjured up" himself. When the park first opened, it featured not only the sunken garden but also mini-golf, a small train, a picnic area and peacocks. It was quite the destination.

It still is a destination for the curious. The place just feels strange. Some people think it feels like a holy place; others think the energy is sinister. There are rumors that the area has been used by Satanists and other occultists for dark ceremonies. At one time, a local Wiccan coven held peaceful gatherings there and adopted the garden as their service project. They built a bridge and cleaned up the garden, but after numerous vandalism incidents, they felt they were unwelcome.

Many people think the location is haunted; they have heard that "bad things" have happened there, or they say horrific rituals occurred in the garden. No one has any specific details. It all just seems to be odd urban legends and strange tales sparked by the unique nature of the location.

Odd, creepy and beautiful all at once, the garden will make the curious mind question why such a place was built. There has to be a reason deeper than just one man's whim.

There are not many details about the creator, Charles Smith, other than that he was a farmer who somehow traveled the world four times and had the money to ship in granite and stone from around the world to build his sunken garden. When he built the garden, it was on his farmland, with his house close by. Years after he passed, the ownership of the garden was in dispute; no one wanted to claim it or take care of it. An article in the *Tri-City Times* from 2019 states that Crestwood Memorial Cemetery, which also owns the Tyrone Memory Garden Cemetery, now owns it.

Pop Of Zero filmed a video at the garden in 2021. They tried to dig deeper into the origins of the garden, but there was not much to find. They flew a drone over the garden and discovered that instead of a circle it is shaped like an eye, and it is sectioned off into eight pieces—eight, like the wheel of the year that pagans and Wiccans use to showcase their four solar festivals and four seasonal festivals. In Christianity, the number eight represents resurrection and rebirth. In Egyptian mythology, several gods had eight disciples—the number of balance and cosmic order.

Could this symbolism point to it being the Eye of Horus or Ra? Peacocks have ties to Egyptian mythology; could there be a specific reason Smith

Tyrone Sunken Garden stone. *Photo by Roxanne Rhoads.*

chose to have peacocks at the location when it first opened? Some of the symbols have ties to the Masons. Could it represent the Eye of Providence, which to the Masons represents the all-seeing eye of God? The Eye of Providence serves as a reminder that humanity's thoughts and deeds are always observed by God, the Great Architect of the Universe. Was Smith a Mason? Did he create something more than a pretty garden? Is there a much deeper meaning and symbology behind his creation?

Smith's obituary stated that his funeral services were "under the auspices of Northville Commandery No. 39 Knights Templars." Well, that answers the Mason question. If his funeral was taken care of by the Knights Templar he was a Mason, which opens up so many more possibilities about the symbolism featured in the garden.

THE LEGEND OF BLOOD ROAD IN METAMORA

Blood Road is a two-mile stretch through a swampy, wooded area of Metamora in Lapeer County. It is interesting that such a small area has so many tall tales attached to it. Could be the name. The word *blood* conjures up all sorts of malicious and murderous thoughts. Numerous stories seek to explain it.

Legend says a man murdered his wife and dumped her in the swamp; now the water and the road turn red like blood. There's a story that there's a grave under the road. There are tales of body-snatching ghosts and vampires. One legend about Blood Road claims that Satanic cultists once used the area to

Blood Road in Metamora. *Photo by Roxanne Rhoads.*

commit sacrifices; so much blood was spilled that it stains the road to this day. How much do you want to bet this legend started during the Satanic Panic of the '80s? Another legend says that if you drive down the road at night, tree branches will fall behind you and the road will turn red.

There's one urban legend about Blood Road that sounds familiar. Versions of it have been shared in remote areas all over the country and have been used as a trope in horror movies and TV shows countless times. This urban legend claims a couple was driving down Blood Road when their car broke down. The man went for help while his girlfriend waited in the car for him to come back. After a while, she heard a strange tapping on the top of the car. Finally, she couldn't take it anymore and had to see what the tapping was. She got out of the car and discovered her boyfriend's dead body strung up in a tree above the car. His dripping blood was the source of the tapping sound.

Numerous haunt websites that include Blood Road mention a traveler who saw figures in long robes chanting around a fire. Some sites share stories from motorists who were chased by large, black shadowy figures or a vehicle that mysteriously vanishes. Sometimes the vehicle is a large truck with bright lights that chases them down the road only to suddenly disappear into the darkness. The stories get more creative as time goes on.

According to HauntedMichigan.net, people have been run off the road by occultists in robes, witnesses have claimed to see ghostly figures rising from the swamps alongside the road and many people have reported mysterious car troubles along that stretch of road. The Haunted Michigan team, better known as Afterlife Road, collected evidence that points to Blood Road being the most haunted road in all of Michigan. They found pentagrams and ritualistic symbols on several trees, they caught a spirit box voice that said "behind you," one of their team members saw a white figure pass behind a tree and the entire team saw an unexplained light alongside the road.

People often think the road might be named Blood because it appears red thanks to its high red clay content. When it rains, the dirt becomes dark red and the puddles can resemble pools of blood. But simple explanations just aren't scary enough; imaginations like to run wild with tales of murder and mayhem. The truth is, the road was named after Norman B. Blood, who was the township supervisor in the 1850s.

CRYBABY BRIDGE (METAMORA)

Crybaby Bridge or Crying Baby Bridge is one of those odd urban legends that everyone talks about, but it doesn't seem to have much merit. There are quite a few bridges nicknamed Crybaby around the United States, all with similar folklore featuring a mother and child where one or both meet an untimely end.

Crybaby Bridge in Metamora. *Photo by Roxanne Rhoads.*

Looking at the Flint River from the Crybaby Bridge in Metamora. *Photo by Roxanne Rhoads.*

The bridge itself isn't named on any map. It's just a rusty little bridge in a wooded area over the Flint River, quite picturesque under the right conditions.

The bridge was built in 1938, and it is located at 42.962976, - 83.240522 in Metamora Township on Wilder Road between East Sutton and Dryden Roads.

The story seems to date back to the 1950s or '60s. One version says that a woman's car stalled over the bridge; she got out of the car to investigate, and when she got back in, her infant was gone. Another version of the story says that the child was a toddler and crawled out of the car. Another version simply states the child disappeared. All of them say that after the woman discovered her child gone, she frantically searched the area and found it drowned in the river below the bridge. Now sometimes you can hear the eerily disembodied cry of a baby or see the ghostly image of the woman searching for her child. One version of the legend even claims you can summon the spirits of the mother and child by parking on the bridge at night and honking your horn three times.

BIBLIOGRAPHY

Books

Barfknecht, Gary W. *Michillaneous*. Petoskey, MI: Friede Publications, 1982.

Fromwiller, Laura, and Jan Gillis. *Oakdale: The Lapeer State Home*. Charleston, SC: Arcadia Publishing, 2014.

Godfrey, Linda S. *The Michigan Dogman: Werewolves and Other Unknown Canines Across the U.S.A.* Eau Claire, WI: Unexplained Research Publishing LLC, 2010.

———. *Weird Michigan*. New York: Union Square & Co., 2006.

Godfrey, Linda S., and Lisa Shiel. *Strange Michigan: More Michigan Weirdness*. Denver, CO: Trails Books, 2008.

McKeon Foster, Marcina. *Stories from the Attic*. Naples, FL: Self-published, 2020.

Radford, Benjamin. *Bad Clowns*. Albuquerque: University of New Mexico Press, 2016.

Shuker, Karl P.N. *Mystery Cats of the World Revisited: Blue Tigers, King Cheetahs, Black Cougars, Spotted Lions, and More*. Charlottesville, VA: Anomalist Books, 2020.

Simon Ammeson, Jane. *Hauntings of the Underground Railroad: Ghosts of the Midwest*. Bloomington: Indiana University Press, 2017.

Taylor, Troy. *Beyond the Grave: The History of America's Most Haunted*. Alton, IL: Whitechapel Productions Press, 2001.

Newspaper and Web Articles

Acosta, Roberto. "New Owners Pumping Life Back into Metamora's Historic White Horse Inn." MLive, November 10, 2014. https://www.mlive.com.

Becker, Justin. "Fenton, MI History: Everything You Need to Know." Tyrone Woods MHC, July 20, 2021. https://tyronewoodsmhc.com.

Benjamin Radford. "Bad Clowns." http://benjaminradford.com.

Bessemer Herald. March 4, 1899. https://www.newspapers.com.

Bienkowski, Brian. "Haunted Michigan Hotel Embraces Its Invisible Invasive Species." *Great Lakes Echo*, October 31, 2011. https://greatlakesecho.org.

Biography. "John Wayne Gacy." https://www.biography.com.

Bonesteel, Joyce. "Attica Hotel Originated as Williams House." *County Press*, March 4, 2018. https://thecountypress.mihomepaper.com.

———. "Attica Said Farewell to Old Hotel." *County Press*, March 21, 2018. https://thecountypress.mihomepaper.com.

———. "Back in the Day." *County Press*, June 29, 2016. https://thecountypress.mihomepaper.com.

———. "Don McCallum Shares Long History with Lapeer City Hospital." *County Press*, February 1, 2015. https://thecountypress.mihomepaper.com.

Bridges, Amos. "Bones Slow to Share Secrets of Their Origin." *News-Leader* (Springfield, MI), July 14, 2014. https://www.news-leader.com.

Caswell, Emily. "Thrill of the Scare." *County Press*, September 27, 2009. https://thecountypress.mihomepaper.com.

City of Lapeer, Michigan. "Downtown Entrance Statements." https://www.ci.lapeer.mi.us.

County Press. "Lapeer County's Mysterious Buildings: Mansion Has Been Columbiaville Landmark for Over 100 Years." June 9, 2018. https://thecountypress.mihomepaper.com.

———. "A Look Back in Time." July 13, 2016. https://thecountypress.mihomepaper.com.

———. "Lucille Annette Rhadigan." May 26, 2019. https://thecountypress.mihomepaper.com.

———. "Past Tense Remains Open Despite Devastating Blaze." August 21, 2011. https://thecountypress.mihomepaper.com.

———. "Search for Local Spirits Leaves Me Empty-Handed." October 21, 2020. https://thecountypress.mihomepaper.com.

Crawford, Kim. "Fenton Family 'Knock It Off Norman." *Flint Journal*, 1979.

Cryptozoologist Loren Coleman. http://lorencoleman.com.

Dell'Amore, Christine. "Extremely Rare White Cougar Highlights a Quirk of the Species." *National Geographic*, December 2020. https://www.nationalgeographic.com.

Detroit Free Press. "Discharged from Confinement." June 26, 1859.

———. "Indicted for Murder." May 11, 1859.

Flint Daily Journal. "Mutilated Body of Mt Morris Girl, Aged 5, Found in Creek." January 30, 1928.

Flint Expatriates. "The Legend of Captain Bubblegum." September 21, 2012. http://www.flintexpats.com.

Flint Journal. "Woman Believed Kidnapped; Grocer Found Slain." January 26, 1976.

Flint Police Operations. "Animal Complaint." Facebook, September 28, 2012. https://www.facebook.com/flintpoliceops.

Foley, Phil. "Divers Recover Doctor's Body from Lake Nepessing." *County Press*, August 19, 2009. https://thecountypress.mihomepaper.com.

———. "Past Tense Country Store Forges Ahead Despite Devastating Fire." *County Press*, October 9, 2011. https://thecountypress.mihomepaper.com.

Foren, John. "A Ghostly Mystery in Metamora." *Flint Journal*, September 30, 2007. https://www.mlive.com.

Genealogy Trails. "Linden, Michigan Genesee County." http://genealogytrails.com.

GhostQuest. "Folklore & Haunted Locations Guide: Metamora Michigan." https://www.ghostquest.net.

Giaimo, Caro. "Stumbling on Skeletons in Old Odd Fellows Lodges: The Fraternal Organization Has Literal Skeletons in Their Closets—and Cupboards, Back Rooms, and Attics." Atlas Obscura, October 30, 2017. https://www.atlasobscura.com.

Goll, Kalpii, and Donald Schram. "The Strange Case of the Nightmare That Revealed a Child Murderer." *Detroit Free Press*, April 18, 1943.

Hall, Christina. "Roseville Police: 2 'Creepy Clowns' Arrested after Terrorizing Teens." *Detroit Free Press*, October 7, 2016. https://www.freep.com.

Haunted Places. "Castaway's Restaurant." https://www.hauntedplaces.org.

Hinds County Gazette. July 3, 1846. https://www.newspapers.com.

Hinds, Julie. "Why Is 'American Horror Story: Cult' Being Set in Michigan? Our Best (or Worst) Guesses." *Detroit Free Press*, August 9, 2017. https://www.freep.com.

Hinterman, Peter. "The History of Genesee County Cities Part Three: Fenton Settled: 1834." *My City Magazine*, March 2020. http://www.mycitymag.com.

———. "The History of Genesee County Cities Part Four: Linden and Argentine County." *My City Magazine*, April 2020. http://www.mycitymag.com.

Historic Farmers Market of Lapeer. "History of Lapeer, Michigan." http://www.historicfarmersmarketoflapeer.com.

Hogan, Vera. "Fenton, Holly and Linden Have Ghostly Tales to Tell." *Tri County Times*, October 29, 2019. https://www.tctimes.com.

Holland Evening Sentinel. "School Boy Finds Body of Woman." January 27, 1976.

Hunsanger, Jacob. "Historical Society Remembers Oakdale." *County Press*, February 27, 2011. https://thecountypress.mihomepaper.com.

Hurley Medical Center. "Historic Milestones." https://www.hurleymc.com.

Ironwood Times. March 11, 1899. https://www.newspapers.com.

Johns, Krystal. "Haunted or Not, Lapeer House Makes for Great Ghost Story." *County Press*, March 16, 2011. https://thecountypress.mihomepaper.com.

———. "Quite a Bit of Activity on the Third Floor: Paranormal Investigators Check Out William Peter Mansion in Columbiaville." *County Press*, March 28, 2012. https://thecountypress.mihomepaper.com.

Ketchum, William E., III. "Flint Legend of 'Captain Bubblegum' Stalks in New Horror Film." MLive, April 13, 2014. https://www.mlive.com.

Lankau, Jay. "The Most Haunted Hospitals in America: Why Spirits Never Left." MedScape, October 29, 2021. https://www.medscape.com.

Lansing State Journal. "Hostage Killed." January 27, 1976.

Lavey, Kathleen. "The Dogman and Other Michigan Mysteries." *Detroit Free Press*, October 21, 2015. https://www.freep.com.

Lethbridge, Alice. "Grave Oversight." *Flint Journal*, July 24, 1983.

———. "Flushing Area Kingdom of Barcelonia Recalled." *Flint Journal*, n.d.

Life at Random. "Largest Timber Wolf Ever Killed & Photograph." August 28, 2008. http://blumenidiot.blogspot.com.

May, Ashley. "Serious or Just a Sick Joke? What We Know About Creepy Clown Reports." *USA Today*, September 28, 2016. https://www.usatoday.com.

McAndrew, Frank T. "Creeped Out by Clowns? This Might Be Why." CNN, October 3, 2016. https://www.cnn.com.

MIGenWeb. "Early History of Lapeer County, Michigan." http://migenweb.org.

MLive. "Creepy Clown Threat Prompts Muskegon Schools to Enter Soft Lockdown." October 3, 2016. https://www.mlive.com.

———. "A Look Back: Crapo Farm Depot in Swartz Creek Was Once the Only Private Farm Depot in North America." February 24, 2011. https://www.mlive.com.

———. "Memories Flow Out at Open House Ahead of Mary Crapo School Closure." May 20, 2018. https://www.mlive.com.

Moralee, Krystal. "Cemeteries Are Like Parks, Adorned with History." *County Press*, October 26, 2019. https://thecountypress.mihomepaper.com.

Mt. Morris City Police Department. "Regarding the Clown Post." Facebook, October 4, 2016. https://www.facebook.com/mtmorriscitypolice.

NatureBoff. "Two Legged Dogman Experiences Database: A Collection of Posts which All Share the Same Dogman Characteristics." Unexplained Mysteries. https://www.unexplained-mysteries.com.

New York Times. "Creepy Clown Sightings in South Carolina Cause a Frenzy." August 31, 2016. https://www.nytimes.com.

Owosso Times. September 28, 1888. https://www.newspapers.com.

Petoskey News-Review. "Drift Yields Body of Hold Up Hostage." January 27, 1976.

Providentia. "Dreaming of a Murder." February 23, 2018. https://drvitelli.typepad.com.

Pugliese, Nicholas. "Paranormal Investigators Search for Ghosts at Columbiaville Mansion." *County Press*, October 3, 2018. https://thecountypress.mihomepaper.com.

Rector, Sylvia. "Help Comes Out of Woodwork to Restore White Horse Inn." *Detroit Free Press*, October 26, 2014. https://www.freep.com.

Ridley, Gary. "Woman in Infamous Internet Love Triangle Slaying Admits Guilt 17 Years Later." MLive, April 28, 2016. https://www.mlive.com.

Robinson, John. "Haunted Michigan: Abandoned Castaways Restaurant in Lapeer." 99.1 WFMK, August 1, 2019. https://99wfmk.com.

———. "Haunted Michigan: Cars Refuse to Move in Pine Run Cemetery." 99.1 WFMK, October 22, 2019. https://99wfmk.com.

———. "Haunted Michigan: Ghosts of Murder Victims May Haunt This Property." 99.1 WFMK, April 10, 2020. https://99wfmk.com.

———. "Haunted Michigan: Ghosts of the White Horse Inn, Metamora." 99.1 FM WFMK, August 14, 2019. https://99wfmk.com.

———. "Haunted Michigan: Three Teens Who Died in a Car Crash Haunt This Graveyard." 99.1 WFMK, October 10, 2017. https://99wfmk.com.

Rocha, Lania. "School Board Discusses Pros and Cons of Demolishing, Renovating Mary Crapo." *Davison Index*, December 9, 2021. https://davisonindex.mihomepaper.com.

—————. "Shhhh, We're Hunting Ghosts Paranormal Investigators Report 'Creepy' Happenings after Exploring Old School." *Swartz Creek View*, March 14, 2019. https://swartzcreekview.mihomepaper.com.

Rosbury, Allison. "The Legacy of James J. Hurley." *My City Magazine*, November 2016. http://www.mycitymag.com.

Rynearson, Jan. "Halloween Immediately Conjures Up Thoughts of Haunted Houses." *Tri County Times*, October 28, 2002. https://www.tctimes.com.

Sandal, Veenu. "Ghosts and Spirits of a Different Kind." *Sunday Guardian Live*, November 3, 2018. https://www.sundayguardianlive.com.

Sands, David. "Michigan Dogman, Mysterious Upright Canine Creature, Haunts State's Backwoods." *HuffPost*, October 26, 2012. https://www.huffpost.com.

Shuker Nature. http://karlshuker.blogspot.com.

St. Joseph Saturday Herald. March 4, 1899. https://www.newspapers.com.

Stokes, Bill. "Monster Cat Stalks the Midwest." *Chicago Tribune*, October 31, 1985. https://www.chicagotribune.com.

Stone, Sharon. "The Linden Hotel Owner Dies: Heartbroken Family to Hold Private Service at a Later Date."

Traverse City Record-Eagle. June 25, 1897. https://www.newspapers.com.

Tri-County Times, February 3, 2021. https://www.tctimes.com.

Tri-County Times. "The Haunted House on High Street: Little Has Changed at Condemned Monastery Over Last 20 Years." May 18, 2013. https://www.tctimes.com.

Unionville Crescent. July 9, 1897. https://www.newspapers.com.

Wildlife Conservation Society. https://www.wcs.org.

Williams, Candace. "Police Probe Alleged Clown Attacks in Sterling Heights." *Detroit News*, October 3, 2016. https://www.detroitnews.com.

Wright, Jerry. "Brent Creek: Its Residents Like It Quiet." *Flint Journal*, September 7, 1979.

Young, Holice, Deb and Clayton. "The History of Genesee County, MI: Chapter XXIX Hurley Hospital Part I." http://www.usgennet.org.

Videos

daryl turcott. "Paranormal Hunt | Lapeer Michigan Castaways Restaurant." YouTube, August 22, 2017. https://youtu.be/iKWWxHFgzJo.

McAndrew Travels. "Terrifying Stories of Lapeer State Home (Oakdale) and Hidden Cemetery." YouTube, October 6, 2021. https://youtu.be/oZ8_WRcQmQI.

ABOUT THE AUTHORS

ROXANNE RHOADS is an author, book publicist, mixed-media crafter, and lover of all things spooky. Her books include *Haunted Flint* and *Pumpkins and Party Themes: 50 DIY Designs to Bring Your Halloween Extravaganza to Life*. She is the owner of Bewitching Book Tours, a virtual book tour and social media marketing company, and she operates a Halloween blog: *A Bewitching Guide to Halloween*. She sells handcrafted jewelry, art and home décor through her Etsy store The Bewitching Cauldron. When not reading or writing, Roxanne loves to craft, plan Halloween adventures and search for unique vintage finds.

JOE SCHIPANI is an integral part of Flint's art community, with ties to local artists, galleries, bookstores, and the Flint Cultural Center. As the executive director of Flint Public Art Project, he has curated an outdoor mural gallery in the city of Flint, with over two hundred murals from artists all around the world. He also serves as one of Flint's Historic District commissioners and loves learning about the history of old buildings. In 2019, he coauthored *Haunted Flint* with Roxanne Rhoads.